MW00964684

AUSTRALIA'S
ABORIGINAL
HERITAGE

About the author

Jean A. Ellis, who grew up in the central west of NSW (Wiradjuri territory), has had a lifelong and deep involvement with Aboriginal people and Aboriginal issues.

She has spent the last twelve years directing research, compiling facts, liaising with the Aboriginal community and studying pertinent historical documents. Jean has for many years been a primary school teacher and has written several books on other subjects including poetry, drama and children's fiction.

As a teacher, she is keenly aware that most Australian students and indeed most Australians need to develop a greater knowledge and understanding of traditional and transitional Aboriginal culture and history.

Jean is also totally committed to raising the awareness of all to the varied abilities and needs of the contemporary Aboriginal community. She is keen to help pave the way towards reconciliation.

Jean lives and teaches in NSW.

Special acknowledgement is given for the information and assistance provided by Robert Ellis, co-author of *Aboriginal Australia Past and Present*.

By the same author

Stories from the Aboriginal Dreamtime
Aboriginal Australia Past and Present
The Multicultural Series
From the Dreamtime — Australian
    Aboriginal Legends
This is the Dreaming — more Australian
    Aboriginal Legends

AUSTRALIA'S
ABORIGINAL
HERITAGE

JEAN A. ELLIS

Collins Dove
A Division of HarperCollins*Publishers*

Published by Collins Dove
A division of HarperCollins*Publishers* (Australia) Pty Ltd
22–24 Joseph Street
North Blackburn Victoria 3130

First published 1994
Designed by John van Loon
Cover design by William Hung
Cover photograph: "Wandamurri, Artist's Area of Birth" by Jimmy Nerrima, courtesy Gallery
Gabrielle Pizzi, Melbourne
Text illustrations by Clive Atkinson, Billy Reid and Biggibilla.

Typeset in Berkeley Old Style by EMS Typesetting

National Library of Australia
cataloguing-in-publication data:

Ellis, Jean A.
  Australia's Aboriginal heritage.

  Includes index.
  ISBN 1 86371 262 3.

  [1]. Aborigines, Australian – History – Juvenile literature. [2]. Aborigines, Australian – Juvenile
  literature. I. Title.

994.0049915

Acknowledgements

We wish to acknowledge Penguin Books Australia Ltd. and Hyland House Publishing
for permission to reproduce the poems in chapter 11.
      Thanks also goes to the Australian Museum, the Mitchell Library (State Library of
N.S.W.), John Fairfax Group P/L and Alcaston House Gallery for the photographs
(acknowledged individually) that appear throughout this book.

CONTENTS

PREFACE

During the 1980s several changes were made regarding the presentation, particularly the publication, of any information relating to Aboriginal culture. Consequently some previously accepted terminology is not now used. Listed below are some of the substitutions that will be found in this and most other contemporary publications.

Former usage	New terms
tribe	group (with subdivisions being referred to as *sections* or *clans*)
race	people
native/s	Aboriginal person or people
walkabout	seasonal migration or journey
witch doctor; magic man	elder or spiritual leader
the Dreamtime	the Dreaming
stories from the Dreamtime	Legends, Aboriginal lore
full blood	Aboriginal ('Aborigine' also still used)
half caste; mixed blood	Aboriginal ('Aborigine' also still used)
tribal life	traditional living

Most Aboriginal people today prefer to be called Koories. This could become an officially accepted, alternative title. In many areas, however, the local terminology is retained; for example, Noongah in Western Australia, Murri in central New South Wales, Jolgnu in the Northern Territory and Wybra in Tasmania.

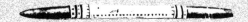

INTRODUCTION

In 1788 an English naval officer, Captain Arthur Phillip, reached the shores of Australia, a land not previously settled by Europeans. He had come to establish and administer a convict settlement.

His naval fleet comprised eleven ships, which transported eleven hundred people in all — convicts, free settlers, soldiers and seamen. The ships sailed for eight months and a day, and covered twenty-three thousand kilometres to reach their destination.

Captain Phillip came to a land that had been referred to as 'Terra nullius', meaning 'land belonging to no one'. This was not the situation at all. People who later came to be known as Aboriginal — a people more than five hundred thousand strong — were occupying this land at this time. They had done so for more than forty thousand years.

Through the aeons of time, these people had successfully divided the large area available so that each individual group had its own special territory; territory that belonged indisputably to those people and they to it.

In 1788, when the First Fleet arrived, there were Aboriginal groups occupying the coastal areas of Australia, the grassy inland plains and the vast mountain areas. Others were living in the arid regions of the interior.

The Aborigines were a people whose economy depended on their given environment plus their own ability to utilise every available commodity. They were a secure people. Their way of life was well ordered and satisfying.

Australia's Aboriginal Heritage gives some insight into their culture and their history, both past and present.

The coverage of necessity is general yet acknowledges that each Aboriginal group has always had, and indeed still maintains, its own spiritual and cultural identity.

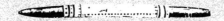

A focus

on the traditional

way of life

The text throughout part 1 of this book is written in the past tense. This has been done of necessity, for easy reading. It is in no way meant to imply that the traditional lifestyle no longer exists. Nothing could be further from the truth. Several thousand people are presently following the traditional pattern, and the numbers are growing constantly. In addition many Aboriginal families who are presently living an assimilated or semi-assimilated life still view many of their ancestral and traditional ties as significant and sacred.

THE
DREAMING

In the beginning

There is no written record of the origin of the Australian Aboriginal people. Historians, archaeologists and anthropologists have made many studies during the past two centuries. They have discovered many relevant facts and have put forward several logical theories concerning early migration, but no conclusive proof of origin has yet resulted.

A study of teachings from the Dreaming — the oral history of the Aboriginal people — is also non-conclusive. For example, many legends indicate that the first Aboriginal people were created in their own territory in ages back beyond human reckoning.

Some Dreaming legends, however, tell of great sea journeys and dramatic new beginnings. These legends could indicate that the ancestors of the Aboriginal race came from across the sea, possibly from continents far distant, such as Asia or Europe. It is equally possible, however, that the legends could be telling of the awesome landscape changes and the subsequent campsite moves which came about for the people of Australia as part of the great ice retreat at the end of the fourth glacial period. No one can be sure.

As the Ice Age finally came to an end, the great ice caps around the world began to melt. As a result the seas everywhere rose considerably and the continent we now know as Australia, like many other land masses, gradually became an island. As a result those people who were here, whoever they were and wherever they had come from, had no choice but to stay.

Carbon-dating processes have proven that there has been continual habitation of Australia for more than forty thousand years; possibly tens of thousands of years longer.

The earliest settlement sites were on the continental shelf, which encircles the Australian coast, and are now, of course, deep under water so archaeological digs cannot be carried out.

As time passed

Archaeologists state that the earliest Aboriginal people were coastal dwellers in the northern areas of Australia. The move southward of several waves of people would have begun gradually as numbers increased and food resources became inadequate. Anthropologists believe that it took several thousand years, possibly longer, for the first people and each subsequent wave to move completely from one end of the continent to the other. It is thought that the first wave was that of a negrito race, small in stature, who ultimately settled in and were finally isolated in the area now known as Tasmania. The physical features of those who came later differed markedly from those of the first people.

A cautious estimate states that in 1788, when Britain established the first European settlement on Australian soil, there were at least five hundred thousand Aboriginal people here, possibly very many more. It is also estimated that there were then about six hundred different groups, each comprising several clans or sections. Between them they spoke several hundred different languages, many of which were variants or dialects of another. These people had, after more than forty thousand years, become an integral part of the land.

Since the dawn of history this vast continent, with its mountains, rivers, plains and beaches, had belonged unequivocally to them and, more importantly, they had belonged to it. Their sacred Dreaming lore, their totem culture and their kinship with nature, way of life, were all expressions of this fact.

This land was theirs. It had always been theirs and it always would be. The continuing faith of these people in their irrefutable Aboriginality, and its subsequent dues and privileges, while it makes them vulnerable is also their greatest strength.

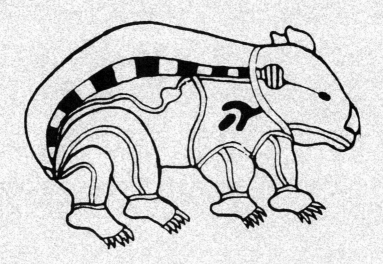

Legends

The legends from the Dreaming, when combined, make a powerful and complex collection that remains unequalled anywhere in the world. The depth of wisdom of the legends, together with their spiritual origin, combined, in traditional times, to give meaning and direction to the lives of all Aboriginal people. It has continued to do so.

Each Aboriginal group had its own separate collection of legends. In each case they had been nurtured and faithfully passed down to succeeding generations since time began. The substance of each and every legend was interwoven with the local history of the totem or sacred emblem of each individual group plus the general lifestyle and personality of those people.

Therefore, the content of the legends varies quite distinctly from one region to another. Overall, however, there are many similarities, such as those given in the following pages.

The Great Creator

The Dreaming legends from all areas of Australia reveal that almost all traditional groups believed in a Supreme Creator. This Great Spirit was known by different names in different areas. Perhaps the best known today are Byamee, Wandjina and Nargacork.

From the legends we learn that in the beginning, the Creative Essence of each area emerged from a void to form the earth's contours, organise the seasons and create the sunshine, the rain and the vegetation. Then, when creation was in complete readiness, the mighty Creator produced the wildlife and finally the first men and women. We learn, too, that the Creator guided chosen people to prepare further and hallow each area for the generations who were to follow.

It was believed that the Great Spirit lived eternally, watching with interest and affection as the Aboriginal people lived out their lives and progressed, each in their given area. There were variations of this belief. For example, in parts of Arnhem Land the people accepted the sun as being the supreme Being and life-giver. The sun was given a female persona. A few groups from scattered regions elevated the Rainbow Serpent into the position of Creator, and in a few areas of Central Australia, the people believed that their own totem ancestors had been responsible for the great initial creation of their area. Many separate legends detail the continuing involvement of the Great Spirit of each area in the lives of the Aboriginal people.

One such legend, told by the Wiradjuri who lived in traditional times in the area now known as Brewarrina, New South Wales, tells us that Byamee, the Creator of that area, sent forth spirit helpers in the guise of men. Their task was to show the people there how to construct fish traps in the river. Solid, circular walls of stone were quickly built, which did indeed help to trap an abundance of fish. The Wiradjuri people created a special corroboree to show their appreciation. They performed this corroboree each time they had a big haul of fish. (Remnants of these fish traps could be seen in the Barwon River at Brewarrina until recent times.)

The eerie, roaring sound of the sacred bullroarer, which was used in traditional ceremonies in most areas, was accepted by many as being the voice of the Creator Spirit calling to his people.

The Rainbow Serpent

Legends that tell of the Rainbow Serpent were among the most widespread. Almost every group throughout the land had some sacred link with this great, mysterious being from the Dreaming. The legends from most areas combine to reveal that the Rainbow Serpent arrived in this land shortly after the great initial creation of the earth, its creatures and the first people. The land was quite flat, it seems, at this time and remained so until the steadily writhing body of the giant Rainbow Serpent began to slide from place to place and in so doing gouged deep gorges, rivers, mountains and valleys in the shape of its body.

The legends from a few separate areas differ from this one. They credit the Rainbow Serpent with the creation of everything. Such legends tell how the Rainbow Serpent went across the land giving birth to many babies. Some of them became men and women while others became the first of the animals, birds, fish and reptiles. The legends tell how the Rainbow Serpent then continued throughout time to provide springs of fresh water as well as enough food and shelter for all of its offspring to prosper.

It was believed that the rainbow seen in the sky after rain was the mirrored reflection of the majestic creature. In most areas it was said that the Rainbow Serpent continued to live on indefinitely in a secret sacred place. It was believed that the Rainbow Serpent did, and would always, watch the affairs of the Aboriginal people of all areas with keen interest.

In the traditional period, most groups paid homage to this great being from the past. Among their tjuringa (sacred) objects were highly decorated, ancient stones which were accepted as being its eggs. They were kept hidden and revealed only during the most sacred ceremonies. Each one was much revered and was passed down from one generation to another. Many of these sacred objects remain hidden in specially selected areas today; their whereabouts are known to only a few initiated people.

The Rainbow Serpent, whose image was once drawn in the sand, cut into the moss of rocks, chipped into sandstone chunks and painted on to bark and in caves all over Australia, was regarded with awe by generations of Aboriginal people right across the land. It is spoken of with great respect even today.

Totem ancestors

From areas right across Australia there are legends that tell how, in the beginning time, men and women could interchange bodies if need be with their own specific totem. For instance, a man whose totem was the magpie could become a magpie for a period of time if he needed or wished. There are legends from many areas that tell how myriad totem ancestors, sometimes in human form, sometimes not, made adventurous journeys across the continent, directly affecting the course of Aboriginal history in mysterious ways. The legendary tracks of the ancestor spirits at times criss-crossed, and each of them left behind living spirits and symbols.

Every aspect of the world of nature — fauna, flora and rocks — were regarded as emanations of some particular group's totem ancestors (also known as spirits). Each individual group felt an unshakeable affinity with its own totem species. This deep and abiding kinship with the ancestral beings welded each group to its own territory, where the totem ancestors were believed to be always present, guarding and guiding.

Specific rituals of increase were practised by all groups. They were especially designed to show the groups' total acceptance of and appreciation for the continuing assistance of the ancestor spirits. Many thousands of

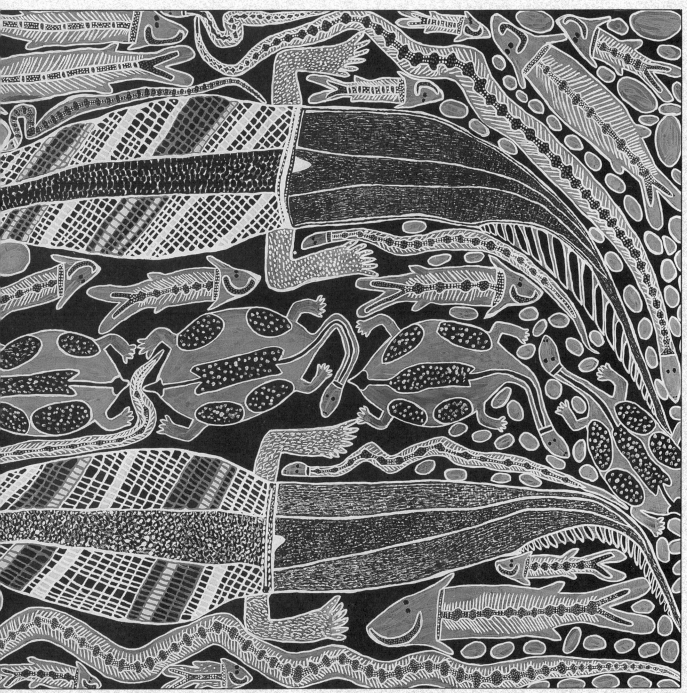

g. 1.1 This painting, *Circumcision and Dead Men's ories (1990)*, by Aboriginal artist Sambo Burra Burra, picts some of the totems such as crocodiles, fish and turtles which were, and still are, sacred to some groups of Aboriginal people.

Courtesy Alcaston House Gallery

Aboriginal people today still hold to their group totem as being sacred: a necessary part of their cultural and spiritual well-being.

Sacred colours

Legends from the Dreaming reveal that most traditional groups had certain colours that were special or sacred to their area. For example, the colour red became a sacred colour to several groups in Central Australia. This belief evolved from a Dreaming legend about Marindi, the dingo.

This legend tells that a giant lizard lived in early times in this area. The giant constantly preyed on the unfortunate people who lived nearby, causing death and distress. Marindi, who was a faithful friend to these people, finally fought the giant lizard. Although the battle was long and vicious, Marindi emerged as the victor.

The legend goes on to explain that the blood of the giant lizard flowed freely and stained the soil in that area. The ancestor spirits were delighted with Marindi's bravery and so, to commemorate this special occasion, they magically caused all the remaining soil in the area to become red as well. This legend explained the massive amount of red ochre which was found in Central Australia. Several groups in the area used the ochre extensively in their art work and body decorations and gained much from bartering to other groups.

As another example, the colour white was regarded as sacred in the area now known as central New South Wales. This belief is explained in a legend about a young man named Wirroowaa. He was the wisest and bravest of the Wiradjuri men who lived at that time in that area.

The legend tells that the Aboriginal people of the area were continually harassed by large herds of giant kangaroos. These giants stood more than three metres tall and were able to crush the life out of defenceless people at will. Wirroowaa asked Byamee, the Great Creator of that area, for help and guidance. Byamee listened well. Then, to test Wirroowaa's skill and bravery, he agreed to help if Wirroowaa would paint himself with white clay. This was a most difficult task because the necessary white clay could only be obtained from the area where the giant kangaroos were actually camped. Wirroowaa, undaunted, bravely accepted the challenge.

To accomplish the task, he smeared goanna fat over his body and then he rolled in the dust until he was covered and hardly distinguishable from the earth. He then selected a leafy branch, which he held above his head as further camouflage. In this guise he cautiously advanced towards the giants and, without being observed, he was finally able to collect the white clay he needed.

Once Wirroowaa was safely back at his camp, he quickly painted his body with the white clay, as he'd been directed. Byamee was very pleased with the young man and straightaway made moves to help the stricken group. To begin with, he sent spirit helpers to the area. It was their task to create a flame from the friction caused by two sticks which had been rubbing together in the breeze. This they did. The breeze fanned the flame and, as expected, it set the dry grass alight, creating a fire that spread quickly.

The members of Wirroowaa's group became alarmed at this point for they had never seen fire before. They hastily gathered their babies and possessions and fled to a high, treeless area. From there they watched as the giant kangaroos began hopping wildly off into the distance. The kangaroos had not seen fire before either so they were quite terrified. As Byamee had planned, every one of the giant creatures left that area, and the Wiradjuri people were never troubled by them again.

The Wiradjuri were much relieved and extremely grateful. Not only were they now rid of the giant kangaroos but also, through Byamee, they had discovered fire with its many uses. From that time on the men of that area painted their bodies with white clay whenever they were planning a special ceremony. This was to show that they always remembered their creator Byamee and his great kindness to them.

Other aspects of the Dreaming

Many legends from various areas tell how animals developed their peculiar traits. For example, one can learn how the kangaroo got its pouch, how the brolga learnt to dance, why the koala does not need to drink and why curlews have a mournful cry etc. Several legends from different areas tell how the stars came to be and why the sun and the moon are up above. One interesting similarity in all such legends, although they vary in story content, is that the sun or its origins is always portrayed as having some form of female link while the moon or its origins is always portrayed as having a male link.

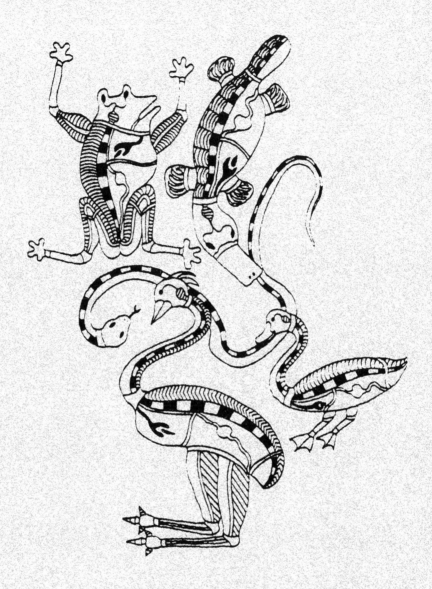

Most of the legends, with all their charisma and drama, were told and retold to all group members, men, women and children. But some sacred legends were for initiated men only. Many of them have never been revealed. The elders of each group usually controlled the retelling of the legends and planned the associated rituals, although women had some authority in this matter. Legends and rites about fertility and the initiation of the young girls were, in most instances, under their command. Indeed, a great proportion of the legends featured women and portrayed them in many interesting circumstances and human relationships.

A study of the Dreaming legends shows clearly that within the mystic cloud of the spirit world there were definite forces of evil or discord as well as good. Most of the discordant spirits or beings, one of which was the bunyip, were said eternally to inhabit caves, dark rock recesses and the deep waterholes of the land. Traditional Aboriginal people of all areas kept well away from any place that was thought to house an evil spirit. Many of the early colonists heard the legends and also chose to keep their distance. Many people today continue to feel very strongly about the existence of the evil spirits or beings from the past.

It is interesting to note that many of the legends from the Dreaming, particularly those concerning great floods, volcanoes, giant prehistoric animals and the changing landscape are now reinforced by contemporary archaeological and anthropological discoveries. However, whatever the ultimate scientific analysis and opinion of Dreaming lore may be, to the Aboriginal people of the traditional period, it was the mainstay of their lives. In all groups, in all areas, it was a continuing, never-questioned reality. To all traditional people, and to many contemporary people as well, every era of the past was echoed in certain aspects of the present and this was how it would be until the end of time. This straightforward yet profound belief, when coupled with their totem tie with nature, gave security and purpose to each group as well as to each individual man, woman and child.

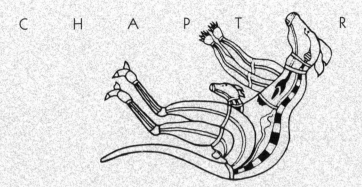

THE TOTEM SYSTEM

Aeons ago, during the beginning time of Aboriginal history, the totem system mystically came into being. Totems have been accepted as part of Aboriginal culture since human reckoning began, and there is a separate totem for each group.

A totem is the acknowledgement of a specific bird, animal, rock or flora species as one's sacred emblem. It is believed that the separate totems were initially designated by ancestor spirits. No group at any stage chose its own totem, and through the centuries it was never changed at any time.

Fig. 2.1 The major Aboriginal groups of mainland Australia in the nineteenth century.

Each person's group, along with their totem, was inherited through the father's line in most instances and through the mother's line in some, as was the case with the Wiradjuri people of New South Wales. All members of any one group shared the same totem. The personal acknowledgement of this totem as sacred was interwoven with and evident in all aspects of each group member's daily life.

Traditional Aboriginal people believed that every bird, animal or rock that belonged to their group's totem species was in fact the actual living spirit of an ancestor. Consequently, each member felt a definite kinship with that species. The totem, if it were a bird or animal, was never hunted or killed for food in that area.

Paintings and carvings of a group's totem were obvious in traditional times in all ceremonies, both sacred and social. A representation of it in some form was also clearly displayed on most implements. The sharing of a totem gave everyone a strong sense of belonging. It also helped create an atmosphere of communal support and loyalty, which was and still is paramount in Aboriginal life. In addition, having different totems gave each separate group a mark of individual identity.

During the course of Aboriginal history, there was need occasionally for a split within some groups. A split became necessary when a group became too large. In such cases the members of the original group would be divided to form two or possibly three smaller clans. Each new clan would then be given its own territory and expected to develop its own resources and become self-sufficient. Each person in each of the new clans would, however, continue to share the original group totem. Over several centuries the separated clans might find themselves living in areas far distant. In some instances they would have even begun speaking in a different dialect because of various speaking taboos. Regardless of the geographic or cultural differences that might have developed, however, the members of the clan would always have a strong feeling of loyalty and kinship towards all others who shared their totem. In difficult times, such as a drought period, the separate clans would assist each other if possible. During prosperous seasons, or for special celebrations such as an initiation ceremony, they would come together socially.

In addition to the group totem which all members and all associated clans shared, each traditional man, woman and child had their own personal totem.

Dreamtime legends from all over Australia tell of ancestors from the Dreaming period who could change at will from their human form to that of their totem species. The legends tell us that the ancestors — sometimes in human form, sometimes not — worked hard to prepare and hallow their given area for the generations to follow. It was accepted that the ancestor spirits were and always would be present there, ready to protect and assist the people of each new generation. Traditional people carried sacred tjuringa stones that united their individual spirits with that of a specific guardian ancestor. Many men and women today carry tjuringa stones at all times.

The totem system was faithfully accepted by all Aboriginal people in all areas at all times during the traditional period. It gave each individual group a sense of pride and purpose. In addition, the totem system helped to cement firmly the deep and abiding spiritual tie between the people of each group and the land to which they belonged. Thousands of people today still hold as sacred their personal totem tie with the land and the Dreaming of the area in which they were born.

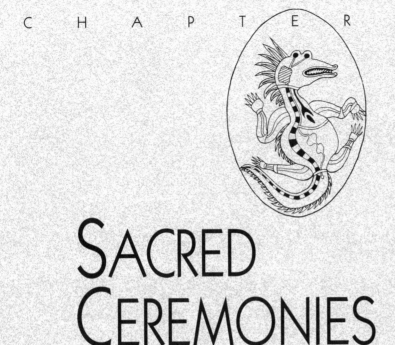

CHAPTER THREE

SACRED CEREMONIES

It was the duty of the chosen elders of each group to organise and control all of the necessary ritual ceremonies. Each ritual ceremony was regarded as sacred, and the preparations for it would begin days ahead.

Elaborate headgear varied for different ceremonies and areas, like the special conical hats, known as waninga, which were used in some areas of northern Australia. Other ornamentation, such as armlets, necklaces and anklets, would be organised ahead of time and held in readiness. Hours would be spent in using special ochres to paint the bodies of the men who would be chiefly involved. The body paintings were always symbolic, and the sacred colour of each given area would be prominent.

Sacred ceremonies included rites of increase, initiation, burial, thanksgiving, hunting magic and rain-making.

Fig. 3.1 Body painting was an important part of the symbolism.

Fig. 3.2 Elaborate ceremonial headgear was worn at ritual ceremonies. These men are dancing an alligator corroboree.

© Australian Museum. Photo: W. Roth. 2108.

The corroboree

During every ceremony there was a specially prepared ritual corroboree, which was accompanied by chanting, clapping and the rhythmic beating of percussion implements. Sacred tjuringa stones and boards, which at other

times were safely hidden from view, would be revealed during a special ceremony. In most areas the freshly decorated bullroarer would be swung aloft to set forth its wild, mysterious cry.

Loud yelling, hissing and mimicking of animal cries was often a feature of corroborees. All non-participating group members and any visitors would join in the chanting, stamping and clapping that accompanied each corroboree. Percussion instruments were used, and boomerangs were often tapped together to reinforce the desired rhythm. In some areas didgeridoos and drums were also used to good effect.

In all areas on all occasions the corroboree became a vibrant, dramatic event. Any member of a group who had the ability to create, choreograph and then teach a corroboree was much praised and respected. Groups would sometimes invite neighbouring clans to watch a well-rehearsed performance.

Initiation ceremonies

Initiation ceremonies were among the most significant of all the sacred ceremonies. No male or female was permitted to marry or become involved in any adult activity until he or she was initiated.

The elders were responsible for the initiation of all the boys of their group. The system varied in different areas, but generally the whole procedure of initiation lasted several months and included several ritual activities. The final ceremony, from which the boy emerged as a man, was the most formal ritual. It usually involved all group members, who were pleased for the boy and celebrated with him.

In all groups each boy was put through some very rigorous trials before the final ceremony. He was put in a situation that caused him to suffer severe pain, hunger, isolation and fear in order to prove that he was ready to face life as an adult. The boys and their families underwent food taboos during this period. In addition it was a time of learning. Over a period of months the boys were each taught much of the history of their forefathers. They were told of sacred duties and responsibilities and further drilled in the techniques of survival, such as how to find water during droughts.

In most instances during the final ceremony one or more teeth would be removed. In addition each boy had several deep cuts made across his back, chest and arms. They were made with sharp flakes of stone and then rubbed with ash to raise them, when healed, above the surface of the skin.

Such scars remained for life. Each boy willingly endured the pain and was proud of his initiation scars for ever after. The boys did not marry for many years after their initiation. Until they married, most of them lived communally in a special reserved section of the camp.

The women prepared the young girls for initiation, but the group elders officiated at the final ceremony. In most groups the testing period for the girls was not quite so severe as that of the boys, but in most areas, teeth were pulled and some form of scarring was also involved. The girls were usually married immediately after initiation was completed. Each girl's husband was chosen for her many years before her initiation.

A section of each initiation ceremony, both that of the boys and the girls, was secret with the young initiates being shown the sacred tjuringa stones and boards, which were normally hidden from view, among other rituals.

The age of initiation varied from early to mid teenage years depending on the individual child and it usually related to the onset of puberty. In most groups the initiation into adulthood was merely the first of several initiations that each person was called on to pass through as their life progressed.

Bora ground celebrations

A bora ground was a sacred area especially and elaborately prepared for an initiation ceremony. It is thought that only the boys were initiated in these specially prepared places. The word *bora* comes from the Kamilaroi language. It means 'belt of manhood', no doubt in reference to the fact that after initiation each young man would wear a loin-cloth-type girdle. It was usually made of fur or hide and decorated with dingo tail tassles or coloured string. The girdle and the initiation ground were called by different names in different areas. *Bora* was used in the nineteenth-century publications as a general term and has continued to be used and accepted as such. The *bora* of Kamilaroi territory were among the first to be noted by white people. After this white people have referred to all such places by this name.

Before each initiation ceremony invitations to other groups were sent in the form of message sticks. They were delivered by the young scouts of the day. Many whole groups travelled long distances, some as far as five hundred kilometres, to attend these special ceremonies. Old rivalries and disputes would be settled or put aside as the various groups arrived. Smoke signals were also sent up, announcing first that the ceremony would be forthcoming, then providing a reassuring and regular direction signal to the travelling groups. Some groups arrived weeks ahead of others. On arrival

Fig. 3.3 A group of men in ceremonial body paint attending an initiation ceremony at a bora ground in Arnhem Land. Note the size of the ceremonial didgeridoo.

© Australian Museum. 15905.

each separate group would select an area and make camp. Many well-planned sporting competitions, such as boomerang-throwing, tree-climbing, duelling, canoe-racing, running and swimming, were organised before and after the main ceremony. Much loud urging and cheering and general high spirits accompanied these activities.

The bora ground gatherings were planned as a time for socialising, relaxation and fun in addition to the more serious, sacred purpose. Each gathering was a highlight in the lives of the groups concerned. Corroboree exhibitions and social dancing by the many groups were also a feature. The coming together of so many people from different regions also provided a great opportunity for trade and barter or arranging future marriages.

There were select and ceremonial bora grounds in all areas. Little evidence is available about the detail of these so the following paragraphs describing the bora grounds of New South Wales are given as an example. Bora grounds were created in this area until the early twentieth century. A bora ground at Darlington Point in the Riverina was the largest and the most ornate of all those for which there is written record. Sadly, this once magnificent outdoor cathedral, like the many others that once existed, has now completely disappeared.

Physical features

Bora grounds usually comprised two large circles, one about thirty metres in diameter, the other exactly half its size. The circles were linked by a path about five hundred metres long. The path always ran due east–west, acknowledging the rising and setting of the sun as marking the days of each person's life.

It is thought that the circles, one smaller leading to a larger, symbolised the broader stream of life that one entered on becoming an adult. In most areas the smaller circle symbolised the constant fertility of women and the never-ending reproduction of human life, while the larger represented the eternal link of people and nature in the broader cycle, or circle, of all creation. The path and the circles (which appear to have been measured exactly) were outlined by the digging of trenches where the lines were to be and then by creating mounds, which were up to thirty centimetres high. The larger circle, the most sacred, contained several decorated stakes, each about 1.5 metres high and having special significance to the ceremony.

Along the walkway there were various carvings, decorations and images, each one deeply etched into the soil. The largest of these usually represented the great Creator Spirit. Other shapes present included replicas of the groups' totem species as well as other birds and animals and numerous

Fig. 3.4 Patterns – with special totem significance – were etched deeply into the soil as part of the preparation of a sacred bora ground.

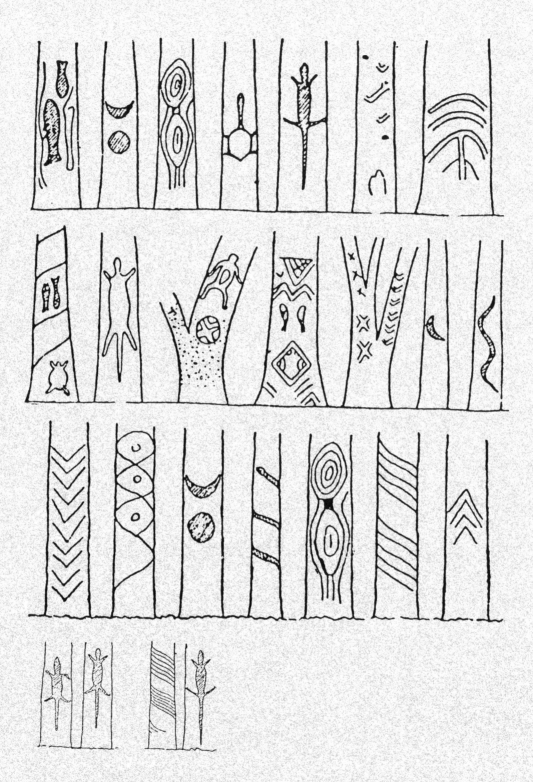

Fig. 3.5 Bora ground tree carvings.

representations of the giant Rainbow Serpent. In addition, fifty or more of the nearby trees — at Darlington Point there were more than a hundred — would be ornately carved, showing many symbolic patterns and many animal shapes. Some represented the totem species of the various groups who would be attending; this was done as a welcoming gesture. Some of the patterning showed the moon, lightning and other natural elements. Intermingled with the carved trees (referred to today as teleteglyphs) were dramatic-looking platform arrangements, which were created by upturning trees and spreading their roots. These were also decorated colourfully and symbolically.

The final ceremony

For the final ceremony the boys who were to be initiated had their bodies painted, usually in red and usually featuring a symbolic pattern, which had some reference to their totem. The officiating elders were usually painted red, white and yellow and wore feathered headgear and colourful body decorations such as armlets and chestbands. Throughout the ceremony the bullroarer would wail, symbolising the voice and presence of their Creator. In addition, several men would maintain a perpetual clapping rhythm by beating two nulla-nullas together. In some areas the didgeridoo was also played.

Everyone present was able to witness and be part of the initial ceremony, which was conducted in the small outer circle, but only the revered elders accompanied the boys along the special path to the very sacred larger circle. Much of the large circle ceremony has to this day been kept secret. It is known, however, to have been a deeply sacred and very significant experience for the boys, sometimes involving circumcision. The total ceremony was always most evocative, well ordered and completely reverent.

Rituals of increase

The continual and natural increase of all species of fish, bird, animal and edible plant life was essential to the lives of all traditional people. It was recognised as a process that must be assisted by performing the correct rituals.

Every separate group organised its own sacred ceremonies, which varied from one area to another. Each ceremony reflected the natural environment of that particular area and the personality of those people. All rituals of increase were organised by the elders, who demanded the total acceptance and compliance of all members of their group.

Within all the groups, the bodies of the elders and the other men involved in dancing the special corroboree would be symbolically painted. Sacred stones and tjuringa objects would be displayed at this time. There was always mime, plus chanting in unison and clapping.

In the arid regions of the interior a main part of the increase ceremony involved crushing stones, which were their totem, and scattering the resultant powder over the countryside. It was believed in this area that stones were symbols left by the spirit ancestors and that the powder would prove to be life-giving. In all areas the ceremony was totally sacred. In most areas the actual procedures have been and are still kept secret from the uninitiated.

Rain-making ceremonies

Rain-making practices were different in form from the increase rites. Rain-making was usually an individual performance by a specific elder who was thought to possess magic powers. It seldom involved whole group participation. Gypsum stones were often used.

Burials

The disposal of the dead, as part of the traditional Aboriginal lifestyle, took several forms, all ceremonial in varying degrees. Customs changed to suit a particular locality, but all ceremonies reflected traditions that had been followed for centuries.

The Aboriginal people, in all areas and through all eras, have lived in closely knit communities, so the social consequences of a death are far reaching. The mortuary ceremonies of all areas involved some form of ritual dancing and chanting, which was repeated, in some instances, for months. In the case of an elder who was held in high esteem the mourning ritual sometimes lasted as long as a year. To those bereaved, the welfare of the deceased's spirit after death was all important. All subsequent ritual activities were planned to appease the spirits so that the journey of the deceased's soul into the spirit world would be made easy.

Specific customs varied from group to group and area to area, but there were many similarities. Throughout most areas of New South Wales and in many other areas, it was common for a widow or widower to wear a cap of clay, which was painted white. Both the cap and the white clay obviously had some spiritual significance that is not generally known today.

Fig. 3.6   Men taking part in a corroboree painted their
bodies in elaborate symbolic patterns.

© Australian Museum. Photo: W. Roth. 2110.

In almost every area mourning rituals involved the cutting of hair and the self-wounding of those who had been closest to the deceased. In most areas rituals also included numerous speaking and eating taboos.

Actual burial procedures varied for the different members of a group. An esteemed elder, or perhaps a young initiated person who had died bravely in tragic circumstances, was afforded the most significant of all ceremonies. In most areas the bodies of these people were mummified through a slow heat process, which sometimes lasted for weeks. During and following this slow process, rituals involving incantation, singing and rhythmic clapping were constant. After many weeks of special ceremonies and taboos, the mummified body would finally be laid to rest in a hallowed place.

In some areas the bodies were encased in bark and placed in prepared hollow logs. In other areas the bodies were securely placed in the branches of tall trees or in sacred caves. In most areas, however, the mummified body was finally buried in a favoured place. If buried, the body was placed in a sitting position, facing the rising sun. A tree close to the grave would, in most instances, be carefully carved in a symbolic pattern and left to mark the grave. Such monuments are referred to today as dendroglyphs.

Less significant people were buried according to one of the methods stated above but without the complicated mummification process or the leaving of a dendroglyph as a grave marker. The personal tjuringa stone was buried with the body. Throughout Tasmania and in a few areas of Queensland the remains of the dead were cremated. In all areas, the name of the recently deceased became taboo.

The people of all traditional groups believed in life after death. Almost all groups believed in ultimate reincarnation. It was generally believed that each person would ultimately be reborn into their own totem group.

Dendroglyphs

In the traditional period each dendroglyph was symbolically carved. In the Central Western area of New South Wales, between the Lachlan and Macquarie River systems, many such trees have been discovered; many are still living. A very fine example of a dendroglyph has been preserved at the primary school in Eugowra, New South Wales.

To create a dendroglyph the bark was first removed with stone axes and chisels, leaving an oval-shaped bare area. A deep, incised pattern was then carefully carved into the sap wood. The pattern always had totem significance to the deceased person and the deceased's group.

Usually one tree marked one grave, but sometimes up to four trees were carved, as is the case with the most famous and best known example

Fig. 3.7a   A dendroglyph in the making. The young man has removed the bark and is carefully carving a deep incised pattern into the sap wood of the tree.

© Australian Museum. Photo: T. Dick. 7822.

Fig. 3.7b   A preserved dendroglyph at Eugowra Primary School, N.S.W.

of dendroglyphing, found at Molong in New South Wales. The trees there mark the grave of Yuranigh who was the scout and friend of Major Mitchell, an English explorer of inland New South Wales in the nineteenth century.

On Melville and Bathurst Islands intricately carved figures, some up to two metres high, were carved as grave markers. The varied influence of people of the Pacific Islands was prevalent in these areas.

37

CHAPTER FOUR

TRADITIONAL ART

The underlying theme of most traditional art, especially that which was meant to be permanent, was sacred and ritual. The Dreaming and the ceremonies that arose from it were a backdrop to most group activities, including art.

For traditional people art was a visual expression of their beliefs. The artists drew their pictures in the sand; they painted them on bark, on trees,

Fig. 4.1 Men preparing stone implements.

© Australian Museum. Photo: T. Dick. 7774.

on their implements and on rock surfaces. They chipped them into moss-covered areas and carved them into timber and sandstone. They created collages, adding feathers, fur and other fine decorations. And they painted their bodies in intricate, colourful patterns.

There is no doubt that art added much to and was a significant feature of the lives of all Aboriginal people. It was much more prevalent than is sometimes thought and stands as a tribute to their faith and creativity.

While most Aboriginal art is accepted as being sacred, it is highly probable, however, that some of it was done as an extended form of storytelling and teaching.

During the traditional period the creation of works of art, whether painted or carved, was the privilege of the men only. The women's artistry was expressed in the making of various artefacts and body decorations. Today, however, there are many female artists, some following the traditional styles, some creating new art forms of their own.

Painting

Traditional artists used brushes made from sticks that had been hammered or chewed until the ends had frayed. Sometimes hair or feathers, tied or glued to a handle, were also used. At times the artist smeared the colour on to the surface with his fingers and at other times pieces of charcoal, slate or hard clay were used in the manner of a pencil.

Colours

In traditional paintings a limited number of colours was used. In some regions certain colours were more prevalent than others. The principal colours throughout were red, yellow, brown, white, black and grey. The red, the yellow and the brown tones were ochre-based. Ochre is a mixture of iron, lime and clay. The white came from lime, special pipe-clay or, in some instances, crushed gypsum rock. In some areas there were deposits of white ochre but they were very rare. The black came from charcoal, and the grey–blue was a mixture of ash and liquids, including gum, which acted as an adhesive.

So significant was art and the necessary colours to these people that the various ochre-producing areas did well from the bartering that resulted. Men travelled long distances from their own areas to obtain what they needed.

During the twentieth century a great many Aboriginal artists, both men and women, have become nationally known and respected. Some contemporary artists have maintained a traditional style, but others have been moved to expand the original concepts. During the past few decades non-traditional crafts, such as batik, screen printing, leather work and pottery, have also been produced professionally.

A study of the traditional art that exists today reveals several very different styles. A brief description of the most prevalent is given below.

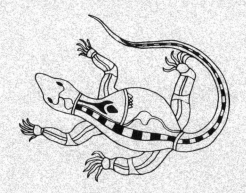

X-ray art

The X-ray style of art was originally found only in the Arnhem Land area, but is now the most readily recognised of all traditional art forms. It reveals the exterior of the creatures portrayed plus the internal organs and the skeleton. It indicates an intimate knowledge of anatomy. In the Arnhem Land area there are huge murals, some more than two hundred metres wide, that show mammals, fish and birds in this way. Each picture contains much added detail as well. The pictures are painted on rocks and the effect is awe-inspiring.

Mimi art

The mimi form of Aboriginal art (from the Greek *mimos*, meaning 'to mime') is perhaps the most graceful of all. Each picture incorporates myriad small match-like figures of men, women and animals. Each is engaged in some obvious activity, so much so that the figures have been referred to in some journals as moving figures.

Paintings featuring them have been found in Arnhem Land in the Kimberleys and in areas throughout eastern Australia, including Cowra, New South Wales. This art form resembles that found in many Pacific Islands and other widely separated places such as South Africa and Spain.

Stencilling

Many pictures that were stencilled during the traditional period are still in existence. This art form is found throughout Australia but is most prolific in the Mootwingie area of western New South Wales. The stencilling of hands was the most common but clearly stencilled feet, various weapons, small animals, reptiles and even, in some areas, a whole human body have been discovered.

The stencilling paint was usually red or white; the significance of these colours is not known.

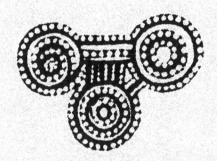

Symbolic art

There is a great amount of original symbolic art still in existence, but unfortunately most of it is not easily interpreted. It is known, however, that each line, shape or change of direction did have special significance to the artist and to those for whom it was originally painted.

Symbolic patterns featured diagonal, parallel or concentric lines. Some were painted on smooth rock surfaces. Others were painted or carved into implements. Many designs were carved into the trunks of living trees, such as those at the bora ground displays or those which were left as grave markers.

Most of the body painting that took place before the special ceremonies was also symbolic. Even if viewed today only as exhibits of patterning, this ancient art form appears most effective in its rhythm and construction.

There are some symbolic styles of painting that can be understood, to a degree. For example, in some paintings small recurring dashes with a straight line through the middle show the trail of a kangaroo with his tail dragging, and a circle with several U shapes on either side is a symbolic picture of several men sitting by a fire.

Symbolic art of various styles was in evidence in most areas, including some rare and mysterious forms that show faces with no mouth or figures surrounded by lines like halos.

Free art

What we have termed 'free' art is that appearing to be a straightforward portrayal of natural features such as trees, rocks, animals, birds and humans seemingly occupied in everyday pursuits. Some of these paintings are very colourful and in some areas cover very large sections of rock. Each example gives a great deal of detail. There is no doubt that such pictures originally epitomised some very special event.

A mystifying facet of this art form is that in several areas, particularly Peak Hill, New South Wales, the paintings vary according to the position of the sun. Strangely, they show much more detail and colour in a dull light than they do in the bright sunlight. Studies are being made to discover the reason for this.

Carving

Timber carving was prevalent in all areas, and many examples on implements, bark slabs and standing trees still exist. The art form exhibited through this medium was usually symbolic.

Rock carving was possibly more widespread than evidence shows, but only a relatively small amount still exists. The most significant of the rock carving finds is that in the Castlereagh area of New South Wales. The many hundreds of engravings found there were carved into the sandstone. They are engravings of the human form and are unique in that they are the only Aboriginal engravings found in Australia which are larger than life-size.

Unfortunately, there is little information available about the Aboriginal people who once inhabited this area, and historians are not sure of the true significance and purpose of their art work. Was it a sacred, formal attempt to show that the spirit of all members of this group would remain in that area, though the people themselves be killed or driven away?

In addition, the sculpting of such objects as dolls, tops and balls was a common practice in all areas. Many tjuringa objects were also sculpted from stone.

Artefacts and other art forms

The making and decorating of implements and utensils often had spiritual and totemic significance. It was also an expression of individual and group creativity and so was always a source of pride.

The copious body decorations, especially the elaborate head pieces of each group, were also an expression of creativity and pride. Body painting was always ordered and symbolic, but the extra ornamentation, comprising feathers, flowers, shells or fur, varied according to the creative flair of individuals or their families. The more sacred the ceremony, the more elaborate would be the decorations. Much care and thought went into each creation.

Some Aboriginal art does not fit into any of the given categories. For example, in rock shelters near Cobar, New South Wales, there is art not evidenced in any other region. It shows many small figures painted directly on top of each other. This conglomerate collection shows hunters, weapons, animals and birds of various kinds, all compacted, quite deliberately. The cultural structure of the Wongaibon group, the members of which had lived in this area for centuries, fell apart soon after white settlement began in the area in the late nineteenth century. Is the art they left perhaps a significant statement showing the tragic end of a way of life that had involved hunters, weapons and animals.

The early Aboriginal people of the Lake Eyre district also created an unusual art display in that they painted several brightly coloured signposts to show the trail that their totem ancestors were said to have taken.

An intriguing but little-known Aboriginal art form being studied at present is picture stone art. Apparently this art form was used as a way of communication and for the recording of facts. It was painted on small smooth-edged river stones. The stones portray very small but quite descriptive illustrations of subjects such as white people and ships, as well as Aboriginal scenes. Some pictures are too small to be seen with the naked eye. Some have been found cemented for lasting protection with a special and very effective resin between slabs of unpainted stone. Future studies of this exciting art form could prove informative.

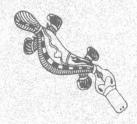

Fig. 4.2 Decorated artefacts from Arnhem Land.

© Australian Museum. Photo: H. Hughes. 9746.

FAMILY LIVING

I n traditional Aboriginal society each family was an extended family with each member giving support of every kind to all other members. Though there were hierarchical obligations to observe, in the main each separate family unit in turn shared whatever they could with other families within that group. Each group was also prepared to share food and give support to all other kindred groups or clans. The constant support that these people so freely gave each other was an accepted part of their everyday life.

Fig. 5.1   Sharing family duties – the men remove bark from a tree for shield-making while the woman and child fish.

© Australian Museum. Photo: T. Dick. 7785.

During the traditional period an Aboriginal family unit consisted of a man, his wife or wives and his children. In most groups the men had only one wife but in many areas, particularly in Queensland, polygamy was accepted. In any area where there were surplus women, some of the men had two wives or at times more. In some areas in some eras the women had more than one husband.

Girls usually entered into marriage immediately after their initiation, which occurred in their early teenage years. Unless they were quite elderly widows were usually remarried soon after the mourning period came to an end to ensure that they stayed in the community and were provided for. The men of most groups were usually well into their twenties before they married.

Marriage

Traditional Aboriginal marriages were nearly always arranged. Sometimes an individual had a say in who was chosen as a second partner but never the first. Each girl was promised to a boy or man while she was very young, sometimes even at birth. It was the chosen male's duty to help keep the girl's family supplied with food, to ensure that she grew up quickly and well. The elders were aware of each forthcoming union and so would sanction it. There was no special ceremony.

All members of all traditional groups followed a very rigid marriage pattern. For this purpose the groups were each divided into two sections, called moieties. *Moiety* is an anthropological term meaning one of two parts or divisions; it is derived from the Latin word *medietas,* meaning half. A moiety is one of the two units into which a tribe or group is divided on the basis of unilateral descent; that is, descended from the parent of one sex, either the father or the mother. In traditional Aboriginal groups it was the duty of each man in moiety 1 to marry a women from moiety 2; this rule had to be obeyed.

In most groups the very structured lineage system was patrilineal; that is, following the male line from father to son. However, a few groups were matrilineal; that is, following the female line from mother to daughter, as was the case with the Wiradjuri people of New South Wales.

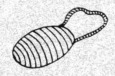

© Australian Museum. Photo: T. Dick. 7765.

If the group was patrilineal the marriage moiety system worked as follows. If a family of two boys and two girls were born into moiety 1, the two boys would automatically stay in that moiety; so too would their sons and their sons' sons, and so on. The two girls, however, would grow up and marry into moiety 2. Any sons born to them would belong to moiety 2 as their fathers had done, but any daughters would marry into moiety 1, or perhaps into moiety 3 or 4 if additional moieties had been established in that area.

In most cases the marriage partners became quite affectionate towards each other. It was the duty of each husband and wife to support each other in their food-gathering roles, and both parents were always very protective towards their children. Divorce was unknown. Both historical records from the colonisation period and stories from the Dreaming lore reveal that some traditional men and women did fall in love with persons other than those chosen to be their marriage partners. If two lovers attempted to run away together they were severely punished by the elders. In some areas breaking the marriage laws was viewed so severely that those found guilty were killed.

Most aspects of traditional Aboriginal life were ordered and ritualistic but none more so than their moiety system of marriage. It most definitely precluded personal choice, yet it was an obviously workable and straightforward system that proved ideal and necessary in communities which were often small and distant from others. The moiety system worked successfully for thousands of years. It continued to work successfully until the colonisation of Australia by Europeans.

Babies and children

The people from most traditional groups believed that babies were pre-existent spirit children who chose their own mothers. When born, the baby's skin was light in colour. If born in summer a mixture of ash and goanna oil was smeared all over the child to protect it from sunburn.

Aboriginal mothers carried their babies with them most of the time. While working with their digging sticks or performing any other chore, the baby would be nearby in a coolamon (a basin-shaped wooden dish) or held by the mother in her free arm. Toddlers often sat on their mother's or father's shoulders.

If a coolamon was used as a cradle, it was filled with sand. This was soft for the baby to lie on and could be changed when necessary. Being rounded, a coolamon could be rocked to and fro if a baby needed soothing. In cold weather the babies were wrapped in kangaroo skin rugs. Each woman breastfed her baby for two or sometimes three years because there was no substitute milk food available.

In all traditional groups the lives of the children were as carefree and happy as possible. They were seldom given specific tasks, but often they assisted the women in food-gathering, helped care for younger children and the aged and gathered firewood when needed.

The children of all eras were treated fondly by all group members and given a great deal of special care and attention by their families. They grew up in an extended family that provided for their welfare at all times and gave them a feeling of security and purpose. It was unlikely that a child in the traditional period would ever be orphaned for, in all groups, the sister of any child's mother was regarded as a second mother and likewise the brother of one's father was in effect a second father.

In most Aboriginal languages the word for *father* also applied to his brother. The children of two sisters or those of two brothers were thought of as brothers and sisters, not cousins, as is the case in contemporary society.

Recreation

The economy and well-being of each traditional Aboriginal group required constant and diligent activity. The continual gathering and preparing of food, the care of children and the aged and the organisation of the special rites and ceremonies, plus the seasonal migration, were ever-present tasks.

Wherever possible, however, social contact plus sporting and swimming activities and contests of many kinds were arranged. Sometimes they were organised within the one group but at other times several

Fig. 5.2 The children often assisted the women in the
gathering of food.

© Australian Museum. Photo: H. Barnes. 1519.

neighbouring or related groups came together. On these occasions there was also much feasting and revelry. Often sacred ceremonies (such as initiation ceremonies) were arranged to coincide with such get-togethers.

Whether or not two or more groups were jointly socialising, traditional people of all groups, weather permitting, spent their evenings in a relaxed atmosphere. The evening meal was the main meal of the day. After it was finished the group members sat around the flickering camp fires. They discussed the day's activities, joked and told stories. Often, too, there was singing and dancing.

In addition to the corroboree, which was an ordered ritual dance, there was much informal dancing. Most of the traditional people, both men and women, were talented dancers. They danced for sheer enjoyment, making each dance as creative and stimulating as possible. At times the dancers simply swayed to the rhythm of the chanting voices and didgeridoos. At other times they imitated the walk and movements of various animals and birds. The people who were not dancing would continue singing and clapping. Women at times danced with an infant balanced on their shoulders. Seldom did the men and women dance together. Usually the men watched as the women danced and vice versa.

Story-telling was also a much enjoyed communal activity. At times sacred legends from the Dreaming were retold. At other times dramatic or humorous representations of current situations were delivered by the most talented story-teller. Quickly drawn sketches often illustrated the stories.

Toys and games

Through aeons of traditional living, the evenings were the time for social contact and relaxation. After the evening meal the adults and children alike sat around the fire, enjoying the cheerful community atmosphere. The children joined in the singing and clapping or sat and listened as the elders told them stories of the mystical Dreaming and the daring deeds of their ancestors. During the day the children played a variety of games and made good use of all the toys provided. Their toys were made from various natural materials, which their parents gathered from the bush.

Traditional children of all eras had a variety of dolls. Some of these were made of stone, flaked and ground into the desired shape, but the majority were fashioned from wood or bark. Others were made of skins, fur side out, tied into the desired shape with strips of sinew. The dolls usually had faces painted on them and necklaces around their necks. In all areas spinning tops were made of stone patiently chipped to form the desired shape.

Ball games were popular. In all areas round smooth-edged stones were used as balls in playing many different games and distance-throwing contests. One of the games was similar to hockey in that two opposing teams were required to drive the ball through the territory of the other. Sometimes balls made from a combination of feathers, hide and hair rolled tightly together were used instead of the rounded stones.

Dancing was another common pastime, and many hours were taken up as the children danced pretend corroborees or imitated the movement and antics of the kangaroo, the emu and other creatures common to their area. The children of all areas had tap sticks and shakers that were bark containers half-filled with pebbles. With these they would together beat out a rhythm while ancient songs were sung and nimble dancers danced. Sometimes two boomerangs would be clapped together.

'Cats in the cradle' games were played with string made from human hair or shredded bark. The children joined the string to make a circle that they looped and relooped over their fingers and toes to form shapes that represented animals or local geographic features.

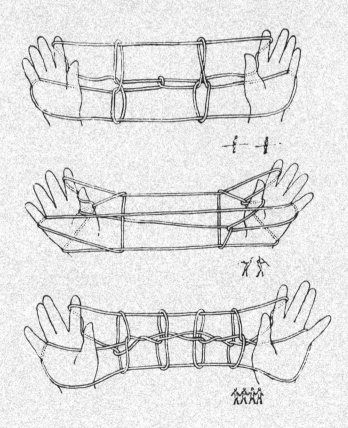

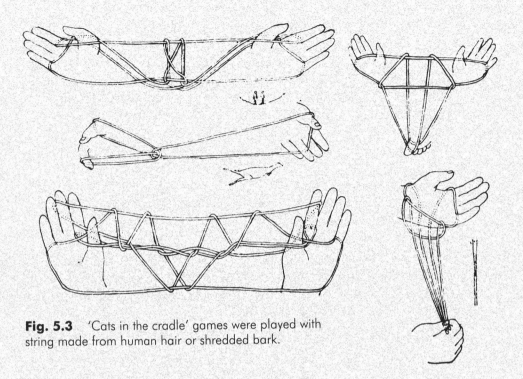

Fig. 5.3 'Cats in the cradle' games were played with string made from human hair or shredded bark.

Most children were talented at drawing. They drew their pictures in the sand or soft dirt areas. Often the pictures would tell a story such as a visual retelling of one of the stories from the Dreaming or a story created by the child.

Much time was also spent on learning and practising the Aboriginal sign language, which was used with considerable speed and dexterity by the members of most groups throughout Australia. The children learned the

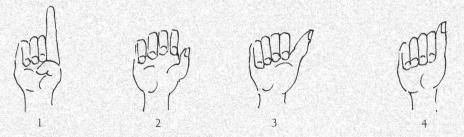

Fig. 5.4 Examples of sign language
1. Who are you?
2. What do you want to know?
3. What is your totem?
4. Water.

gestures, which were usually made with their hands, arms or head, and then enjoyed communicating this way.

Both boys and girls of all areas enjoyed climbing and found the practice beneficial in later years as they gathered food. Hide-and-seek was also popular.

Bowling games were also prevalent in all areas. The children used their stone or soft feather balls for bowling and they also made and used simple bark discs. The bark, usually from a eucalyptus tree, was cut into a circular shape about fifteen to thirty centimetres across. Sometimes as the disc was sent rolling along the ground, the children would attempt to spear it. Other target games were also played, including one that involved a toy made from hide, fur and hair, which was called different names in different areas but looked something like a small mouse. The boys threw spears, stones and sticks at it as it was sent skimming along a flat surface.

Swimming, canoeing and all associated water games, including fishing, were the source of much fun all along the coast and at inland waterways. Naturally too, many hours were spent with the children of all areas learning how to make and use the various stone, wooden and bone implements used by their parents.

Running, chasing and wrestling games were part of the entertainment in all areas. Traditional groups were very competitive, and contests that featured these and other activities were held for the adults as well as the children. Boomerang-throwing contests as well as swimming and canoe-racing were organised for children and adults. Sporting competitions between neighbouring or associated groups were arranged as often as circumstances permitted.

Clothing

Most traditional people from all areas spent much of their time unclad, which was possible in such a temperate climate and convenient when people were on the move, as they often were. In many groups the men wore 'girdles' of fur or twine. The men and women of each group wore decorations of many kinds, including armbands, necklaces and headgear. Some were worn every day, others for special ceremonies only. In some areas the girls preparing for their initiation wore special decorations.

On Melville and Bathurst Islands, and on Groote Eylandt, the women often wore apron arrangements made from woven leaves or possum skins. In Arnhem Land the women wore skirts plaited from pandanus leaves.

In all areas the Aboriginal people smeared their children, and sometimes themselves, with oil as a protection against the elements. In the cold months they wore kangaroo or possum skin cloaks. They wore the fur side in. Babies of all areas were wrapped in fur rugs. In some areas, particularly where there were rocky sections, shoes of a kind were made from animal hides or bark.

Language

In January 1788, when Governor Phillip arrived with the First Fleet, there were an estimated five hundred thousand Aboriginal people in Australia, possibly a great many more. Between them, they spoke more than five hundred different languages, many of which were variants or dialects of another.

In early times the new white race made little attempt to learn or record these languages. During the second half of the nineteenth century a more serious effort was made, but overall the results were disappointing. Consequently, many of the five hundred languages spoken have now been completely lost, and there is only a sketchy record of most others. No more than fifty Aboriginal languages are functional today; that is, being spoken by young children.

Of the languages on record we find that, although the words varied from group to group, there were some features from all areas that remained constant. For example, the name of a recently deceased person and articles or situations relating to that person became taboo.

It was the Aboriginal custom, in most circumstances, to use as few words as possible. One Aboriginal word often translated into a quite lengthy English phrase. For instance, the word meaning *animal* would simply be pronounced slightly differently or given a prefix to imply that the particular animal in question was running, drinking water, up a tree or on the alert. Words relating to sacred issues were seldom spoken in front of the uninitiated so whole sections of some languages, otherwise recorded, are missing.

The sounds *s, z* and *h* do not appear to have been used in any area. There is a repetitious, lyrical quality within most Aboriginal languages that gives them a pleasant, musical sound.

Sign language was a very effective and much used method of communication. One sign language was used and clearly understood by the members of most groups in all areas of mainland Australia. This was most beneficial when different groups came together socially. It was also helpful during trading expeditions and while hunting.

Fig. 5.5   In the colder months, the people of all groups wore fur cloaks.

Mitchell Library, State Library of N.S.W.

Words from the Wiradjuri dialects

Several hundred words known to the Wiradjuri people of central New South Wales appear in the appendix to this book. Although the list is reliable, it is not intended to be viewed as a comprehensive study of the language. It is a word list from several different sections of the Wiradjuri. It includes many present-day town and property names, including Canberra.

Fig. 5.6 An Aboriginal mother and child.
This illustration was commissioned and exhibited during the 'International Year of the Child' (1979).

Artist: Billy Reid.

Fig. 6.1 Men and women gathering shellfish at the water's edge.

© Australian Museum. Photo: T. Dick. 7736.

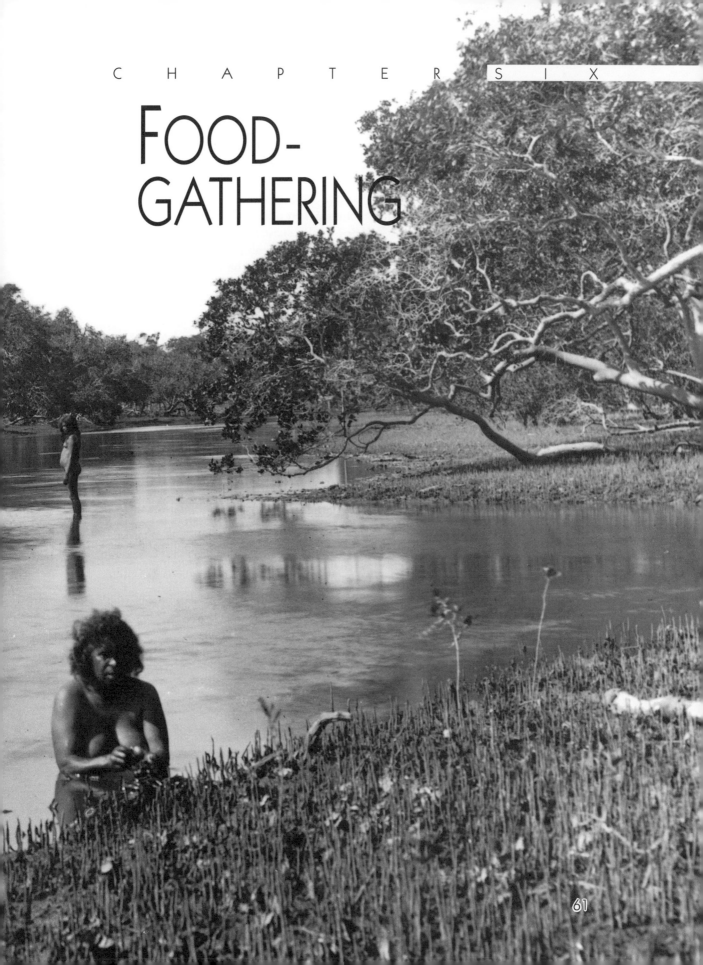

FOOD-GATHERING

Before the Europeans came the Aboriginal economy depended on the natural, available food and the skill of each particular group in obtaining it. And, as in all aspects of traditional life, the local geography and climate governed the way each group sustained itself. For instance, the people who lived in the arid desert areas of Central Australia had to use certain skills and techniques to obtain their food, while those who lived on the well-grassed plains or the coastal areas naturally had to use different skills. In all areas their knowledge and ability were adapted to suit their own area. No one had an easy task. Most of the available food could not be stored and had to be gathered anew every day.

Aboriginal people of all groups found and adapted themselves to eating many different plants, animals, birds and insects, thus varying their diet considerably and ensuring that no single food was eaten out of existence.

The basic food of all mainland groups included bread-like 'dampers' made from the flour of various seeds. They also ate wild fruit, nuts, honey, various leaves, yams and other edible roots, kangaroos, possums and all other mammals as well as birds and their eggs. Additional foods included some bark species, moths, witchetty grubs, lizards, snakes, spiny anteaters and goannas. When available they added turtles, mussels, crabs, shellfish, many varieties of fish and eels, aquatic birds and, on occasion, manna and lerp. (Manna is a white sugary deposit left by insects while feeding, and lerps are the tiny cocoons made from the manna. At times several kilograms of manna and lerp could be obtained from a single tree.)

All meat was cooked before it was eaten. Water, sometimes sweetened with honey, was the only cold beverage. A hot tea-like drink was made by boiling eucalyptus or other pungent leaves in water.

In all groups both men and women had specific duties, and the aged and very young assisted when possible. The greater part of their lives was in some way connected with the gathering of food. There was always time, however, for relaxation and lots of social contact.

Food-gathering roles of women and men

The role of traditional women in the task of supplying food was to gather and to cook the smaller creatures and the plant-associated foods. In most groups the women were in fact the mainstay of their families in providing food.

Fig. 6.2 Although it was usually the women's task to collect food from plants, this picture shows two Aboriginal men collecting zambla nuts from a palm tree.

© Australian Museum. Photo: T. Dick. 7715.

Along the coastal areas the women could gather shellfish, lobsters, pipis and crabs. Those who lived inland looked for freshwater mussels and yabbies, which were much relished. When possible, the women gathered large supplies of spinifex and other seeds, including those from the kurrajong and wattle trees. They later disposed of the husks and then ground them into flour, which they then mixed with water. The resultant dough was kneaded into shape and cooked on a shelf of hot rocks, which had been placed in a special part of the fire for the cooking of such items. This damper-type food was an important part of the diet of all mainland people.

With their digging sticks and wooden shovels the women, helped by the children, spent hours each day searching in the ground for edible roots, yams and witchetty grubs. (Witchetty grubs are the larvae of a beetle, high in protein, which grows to be about five centimetres long.) Women also fossicked in the soil, beneath the bark of trees and in hollow deadwood for insects of various kinds, plus snakes and lizards. Where possible, they gathered waterlily stalks, which had a texture and a taste similar to celery. Always, too, the women were on the lookout for the nests of wild bees. If they could catch a bee they would attach a small white feather to it, set it free and then follow it to its nest. Honeycomb was considered a delicacy. Honey, if plentiful, was used to sweeten water as well as to heal burns.

In addition, the women spent much time in making the string needed in the manufacture of fishing nets, hunting snares and dilly bags. The 'string' was made from sinews, vines and certain kinds of bark. The bark had to be hammered for some time before the shreds were rolled into strips. The women also helped to make some of the nets and bags.

Most of the women were as adept as the men in climbing trees and, when necessary, they helped the men capture small tree-living animals, birds and their eggs. In many areas the women, like the men, fished from canoes in the shallow waters. The women also swam and dived deep to spear fish. They fished mostly at night or in the early morning. In the southern coastal regions, including Tasmania, the women were extremely talented at catching large sea mammals, such as seals. They also helped at times to corner the larger animals, such as kangaroos, ready for the hunters to spear. They gathered whatever wild fruits, nuts, berries and edible leaves were available.

In most instances the women of the traditional era worked as a group, the young helping the old. Food-gathering was mostly a happy, communal activity for them.

The basic role of traditional men in the task of gathering food was as hunters and fishermen. When hunting, the men used their knowledge of

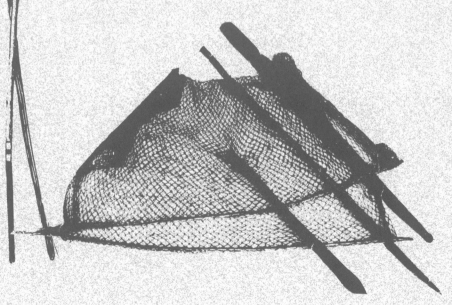

bushlore, their agility and their unique tracking skills as they stalked their prey. When fishing, they used their strength, their ability to stay underwater for long periods and their deftness to good effect. They also devised and made use of numerous tricks and traps, as we shall see. At times each man hunted alone, but mainly they hunted as a team. They hunted or fished during the day, in the very early morning or even at night if an occasion warranted it.

In addition to hunting the men spent much of their time manufacturing the many weapons and tools they needed. It was also the men in most areas who built and maintained the large fires. The men did much of the cooking, particularly that of the larger animals. When necessary, they created fire through the friction generated by rubbing two sticks together.

Tools and weapons

The tools used by women in all areas for gathering food included digging sticks and (in most groups) wooden spades. Coolamons of all sizes, some made of bark, some of wood, were in constant use in all areas. Food gathered was carried back to camp and stored in them until needed. Women everywhere used dilly bags made of string as carry bags. Some in northern areas had baskets woven from reeds. They used grinding stones, one large and flat, and a smaller one, smooth-edged and rounded, to grind grass seeds into flour. They used stone axes and bone awls to chip and gouge into bark and deadwood. The women also used small spears with several sharpened prongs, some shell tipped, for fishing and as cooking tools.

The men of all mainland groups made use of many weapons and tools as they sought to keep their families supplied with meat. Stone axes, chisels, picks and hammers were used in many ways, as were bone knives and awls. Waddies (heavy wooden war clubs), spades, many varieties of spears, woomeras (notched throwing sticks that enabled spears to be thrown further) and boomerangs were fashioned from timber and used extensively. In addition they made fishing nets, some wide enough to reach right across a stream, and snares and ropes of different sizes. Aboriginal men who lived near waterways also constructed much-needed bark and dugout canoes.

Some of the desperation, the drama and the triumph of traditional hunters was revealed in their art and in the Dreaming legends. Down through the centuries their hunting practices remained complex, controlled and constant.

Hunting techniques

Hunting methods and techniques of traditional Aborigines varied according to geographic conditions and the skill of each group or clan, but most procedures were widespread.

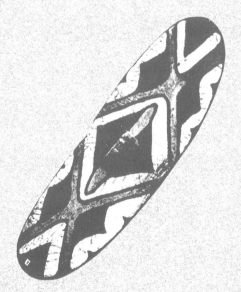

Fig. 6.3 Spears were among the many weapons used to hunt animals for food.

© Australian Museum. Photo: T. Dick. 7817.

Catching fish

Many fish were caught by men who stood in shallow water and simply speared or clubbed them on sight. Some fishermen and women, particularly those in northern areas, fished with a hook and line. The hooks were made of bone, stone or shell.

Large string nets complete with stone weights were used in many coastal and inland waterways. The nets would be lowered into the deepest water. After a time, the nets would be raised quickly, and the fish in them would be caught. Sometimes the water of a stream was deliberately stirred up until it was quite muddy. Stupefied fish would then come to the surface where they could be quickly clubbed or speared. Sometimes poison roots, such as the tjarmo from North Queensland, were powdered and fed to fish. Once poisoned, the fish would float to the surface. The poison did not affect the people.

Aboriginal men and, in most areas, women spent much time fishing from their canoes, spearing any fish that came to the surface, or else swimming underwater where they transfixed any that came near. In the colder months a fire would be lit on a base of clay on the floor of the canoe to give light as well as warmth during night fishing.

Permanent stone walls that created a chain of separate pools were built along some river systems. The walls consisted of piles of rocks. Fish became trapped in the pools whenever the water rose quickly and then fell. Walls

Fig. 6.4 Fishing was often done at night or in the early morning. These Aboriginal men are using nets.

© Australian Museum. Photo: T. Dick. 2169.

Fig. 6.5 Bark canoes were used for fishing and for recreation in all coastal areas and all inland waterways.

© Australian Museum. Photo: T. Dick. 7810.

such as this existed in the Barwon River, the Katherine River and possibly also in many other areas. Similar walls were often constructed in tidal areas. At times hollow logs, blocked at one end, were placed in inland waterways. Men or women would then drag clumps of reeds along the water bed. This would frighten the fish, causing them to seek refuge in the logs where they would be trapped.

During flood times, fish were sometimes stranded when the water receded. The Aboriginal men dug trenches and holes in readiness for them.

Catching birds

Many birds were trapped while attempting to drink, particularly birds like parrots and pigeons that travel as a flock. A hunter would place a net in position before the birds arrived. When the time was right the net would be dropped and many of them would be caught.

At times, gum or some other sticky substance was placed on the branches of trees where birds were known to rest. After a time any birds that had landed there were unable to rise, thus enabling a waiting hunter to capture them.

Nets were often placed in the long straight sections of rivers and creeks where ducks abounded. The ducks would then be disturbed by a low-flying object, usually a boomerang. More carefully aimed, low-flying boomerangs would follow so that the ducks were driven forward but kept low. Eventually they would come to the net and become entangled.

A very common practice in the catching of water birds was for a man to wade or swim slowly downstream with a leaf-covered branch covering his head. When he came near the unsuspecting birds, he would dive underwater and grab several of them by the legs. The birds would then be held underwater and drowned. Turtles resting on rocks were often victims of this same method of capture.

Loop snares made of string were also used. First, seed was placed in a certain area. Then, as soon as a bird began to peck at the seed, a well-positioned loop would catch it around the leg or neck. Men who lived in swampy areas, such as in Arnhem Land, were able to catch hundreds of magpie geese and other marsh birds in surprise attacks during the breeding and nesting season. Another common practice was to sprinkle seed or meat on the roof of one's gunyah (a hut made of boughs and bark). Wild ducks, crows or galahs that pecked at the food would be grabbed by the leg from below.

Aboriginal men perfected the art of tree climbing. They could climb smaller trees of ten to twenty metres high by placing both hands and both

© Australian Museum.

feet around the trunk. Then, with a series of whole-body jumping movements, they would quickly reach the lowest hanging branch. On larger trees more than thirty metres high a series of toe-holds were cut in a zigzag pattern enabling the climber to hold on to the bark above while still keeping a firm foothold. Sometimes strong ropes were hoisted up on to the highest branches, and a climber would pull himself up with it or steady himself against it. This ability to climb even the highest tree enabled the men to capture many of the smaller mammals in addition to catching birds and raiding their nests.

Catching animals

It is interesting to note that the Aboriginal people did not hunt or kill any animal for sport. They did not cage them, use them sacrificially or scientifically. They killed only those animals needed for food and only when it was necessary. They knew a lot about and had a deep-seated respect for each living creature, believing that each one, like themselves, had its special place in the overall plan of creation and life.

Aboriginal men hunted always with the wind blowing towards them and away from the animals so that the animals would not pick up their scent. In addition, they hunted as often as possible with the sun at their backs.

A form of animal husbandry was practised in traditional times whereby the men would cut holes in hollow trees for possums to nest in. Such trees were marked and at a later date would be raided. During the raid a lighted stick would be placed inside the hole, sending smoke up the centre like a chimney. The confused possums would run out on a limb where a waiting hunter would capture them.

Snakes, lizards and small animals were often chased into hollow logs, and hooked sticks were used to extract them. Kangaroo rats, wombats, echidnas and other hole-digging creatures were smoked or dug out and then clubbed.

Bandicoots, flying foxes and other nocturnal creatures were also caught for food. Sometimes they were victims of a surprise daylight attack. At other times, loop snares or nets were used to catch them after they had been enticed to an area by a bait of food.

Koalas were taboo to several Aboriginal groups — due to a widespread belief that to harm a koala would cause a drought — but in some areas they

Fig. 6.6 Aboriginal men mastered the art of tree-climbing to capture smaller mammals and birds. The women were also adept at climbing.

Photo: T. Dick. 7723.

Fig. 6.7 Koalas were taboo in some areas of Australia. It was believed that the spirit ancestors of the koala would cause a drought if one of their number was harmed.

© Australian Museum, Photo: T. Dick. 7835.

too were captured for food. The men would climb a tree and shake the narrow branches until the animals fell. Hunters waiting below would catch them.

It was common practice by all groups to set animal traps on the best-known waterhole tracks. Traps took the form of a fence-like barricade made of bushes and saplings. The animals would be startled and made to run through openings in the fence and thence into the cone-shaped sapling traps or nets which had been earlier placed behind them.

The kangaroo

The kangaroo was hunted in all areas. Kangaroos are mainly nocturnal animals. They were often hunted during the heat of the midday sun for they were more easily caught when drowsy. They were the largest of the animals hunted and were of great significance to the way of life of all traditional Aboriginal groups. The reasons for this were as follows.

Kangaroos were a major source of meat, and their bones were useful in the making of many implements. Their hide was fashioned into water carriers, rugs and cloaks, and babies were wrapped in or lain on kangaroo skins, fur side up. Strips of the hide and sinews from the tail were used as string for lacing large hides together, making nets and binding axe heads to their handles.

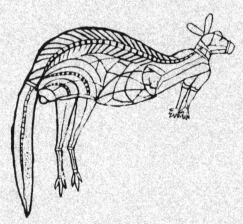

Apart from the straightforward hunt, traditional men used many tricks to catch kangaroos. One method in all areas, including Tasmania, was the horseshoe of fire. The animals, realising they were trapped, would attempt to escape through the unburnt section and so become easy prey for the hunter with his spear.

Another method made use of a helpful geographic feature. Quite often a right-angled bend in a river or creek has one high bank and one low. At times the hunters would conceal themselves on the high bank, which gave them a perfect view of the lower one. When the kangaroos came to drink, usually at sunset, they were greeted by a rain of spears, thus ensuring that everyone in the hunters' camp had meat for the next few days.

The hunters of most groups would sometimes disguise themselves with branches and then stalk their prey, having covered their bodies with clay to hide their human scent. They would creep slowly up on the kangaroos and then, when close enough, they would attack. Many unsuspecting wallabies, emus and brolgas were also caught in this manner.

Hunting rituals

Hunting ritual ceremonies differed in different areas, but all traditional groups believed in the conjuring of hunting magic. Sometimes individual hunters performed personal rituals, as suggested by the elders, which were designed to bring them individually into favour with the spirits. At other times the whole group communally followed a sacred ritual program.

Sacred, communal ceremonies preceded almost every large or special hunting expedition. The men would paint their bodies symbolically and sacred ornaments would be displayed. A corroboree would be danced with the men miming and chanting the stories of the past. Usually the women tapped their thighs or clapped their hands rhythmically in accompaniment. In some areas the didgeridoo would be played.

It was hoped that the ceremony would create powerful spirit forces that would render all animals spellbound, making them wander helplessly and therefore be easily caught.

Additional ceremonies and celebrations involving corroboree dancing also occurred when the hunters returned triumphantly to camp. Much of the art of the Aboriginal people portrays the skill and the triumph of their hunters.

Food-related customs

Gathering and preparing food took up much of each day in the lives of traditional people. Many of their spiritual beliefs and ritual ceremonies were also in some way connected with obtaining food. The need for food was a constant and always pressing priority.

Cooking procedures

Cooking procedures varied little from group to group or from era to era. The main meal of the day was the evening meal. The fires were lit early, and the meal was left to cook as members of the group relaxed and socialised. After the meal there would be storytelling, singing and dancing as fires lit up the area and cast a cheery glow.

In most groups, the men did a large proportion of the cooking, particularly that of the larger animals, and the women were responsible for the roasting of the smaller animals or birds and the making of dampers. The children and the old people assisted by gathering firewood.

The meat was sometimes barbecued over an open fire. At other times, however, if circumstances permitted, it was cooked in a huge earth oven, which provided a sophisticated cooking method whereby heat was well controlled and the meat was cooked thoroughly and evenly. To make such an oven, a long trench had to be dug and partly filled with stones, pieces of white anthill or pieces of clay. Once built, the oven became a permanent structure. Each group would build several earth ovens at different points on their migratory route. With slight modification, they could be reused each time the group returned to that spot. Some were in existence for centuries. A large fire would be lit in readiness for cooking in such an oven and allowed to burn until only hot coals remained. They were then raked back, and the animal or animals to be cooked would be placed on top of the hot stones. Sand or old ashes were then placed on top of the carcass and another fire was lit above. Sometimes a vent was left, through which water was poured from time to time. The steam assisted the cooking.

Often eucalyptus leaves were used to flavour the meat as it cooked. Usually the fur was singed off before the carcass was laid on the coals. Sometimes animals were cooked intact, but mostly the entrails were removed and replaced with hot stones, which hurried the cooking along. Several hours, sometimes a whole day, were needed to cook large amounts of meat in this way.

Another cooking method was boiling. Large shells and stones with a natural or handmade concave depression were used as utensils for boiling. Various leaves, nuts, species of bark, berries and fruits were boiled at times. So were some medicinal preparations.

Small items of food collected were often eaten individually or by a family, but strict hierarchical rules governed the distribution of meat and other major foods.

Many Aboriginal middens can still be seen today, particularly along the eastern coastline, including Tasmania, and in inland New South Wales. (A midden is a huge mound formed over hundreds of years from the remains of campfires and foodstuffs, as well as bones, shells and pieces of clay.) One such heap at Mirrinyonga, in the lower Murray region, is forty metres long, sixteen metres wide and four metres thick. No doubt it was once even larger! Many early settlers used the compacted material from the old middens for building purposes. Many present-day farmers are quite unaware, however, that what might appear now to be just a raised section of earth could well once have been an earth oven and midden and, therefore, the centre of an Aboriginal campsite.

Food taboos

Food taboos were practised by all groups but varied greatly in degree and content. Each taboo had a ritual basis, and some form of taboo was observed by every person at some time during their lifetime. Children were excluded from all food taboos until they reached initiation age. All groups made their totem animal or bird taboo, and the taboo species could not be eaten under any circumstances.

In most groups the young male initiate and his parents were forbidden to eat the more common mammals, those he could easily catch, until his final initiation ceremony was performed. Similarly, a young girl and her parents were restricted while she was between different stages of her initiation. This taboo was designed to stimulate initiative. The members of most groups practised general fasting or specific food taboos during periods of mourning. Some groups forbade pregnant women to eat animals that burrowed. In some areas the father-to-be was also affected by certain food taboos.

All of these restrictions, and others, usually of the most common foods and often lasting for months, must have caused considerable hardship, but a taboo was always adhered to. Strict obedience was necessary in these and all other ritual matters. Severe penalties, real and imagined, awaited those who dared to defy them. Food taboos became an incidental but actual form of food conservation.

Drought periods

Droughts have plagued Australia for centuries. Most native animals are grass-eating and, as a drought period lengthened, finding food became difficult.

Drought might have been one of the reasons why the prehistoric creatures such as the diprotodon and the giant kangaroo died out.

During a drought period in the traditional era there was no water for washing or for cooling play, but almost always the Aboriginal people were able to find enough for their drinking needs. Even in the driest areas of Australia there are permanent waterholes and underground springs if one knows where and how to find them. The traditional Aboriginal men could do so. If the situation became desperate they were able to drain water from the roots of trees, most especially from the coolibah eucalypts.

Part of the initiation ceremony of young men involved the learning in a chant form of where and how best to discover hidden water systems. Water was the only drink available in the traditional era, so finding it in drought periods was all-important. (Sometimes it was sweetened with honey or mixed crushed leaves to make it like a herbal tea.)

However, finding food during drought periods was not as difficult as one might expect, for the animals and birds, weakened by hunger and thirst, became easy prey for the experienced hunters. Plant-associated foods became less plentiful.

The period immediately following a drought was more difficult for the Aboriginal people, as there were then far fewer animals around and those which had survived were once more fit and harder to catch. In addition, the various grasses and trees took a season or so before again producing their normal supply of seeds and fruits.

Conservation

Aboriginal people practised many forms of conservation, the most significant being their regular seasonal migration. The migratory circuit of each group followed the same route and usually took place in the same seasons of each successive year. Naturally grasses, fruit, insects and animals would build up in one area while the group was absent in another. The migratory cycle continued for the members of each group all the days of their lives. Each group had its own territory and seldom infringed the territory of another group without an invitation. The people in coastal areas and in the tropics did not need to move on as constantly as others, but some groups, such as those in the dry areas of Central Australia, were on the move frequently.

By varying their diet to include almost everything in the area that was at all edible, the Aboriginal people ensured that the one or two favoured food items would not cease to exist. All groups were careful to leave enough seeds in each area to ensure regrowth of the grasses needed. Many groups scattered seeds. Unless food was desperately short the hunters did not kill the young of any species, nor a female which was still raising her young. If a bird's nest was robbed of eggs, some would always be left to hatch. Grassland areas were seasonally burnt off in an effort to stimulate germination and regrowth and so encourage more animals to the area.

The traditional people of all areas employed preserving skills where possible. The flesh of some of the larger animals was sometimes cut into strips and dried for future use. Wild stone fruits such as quandongs were dried in the sun and stored. They would be later soaked and pounded before being eaten. Nuts were sometimes buried in the sand for future use. Turtle and birds' eggs were pulped, dried and stored in a protected place. However preserving food was not always of much benefit. Often food could not be stored satisfactorily and so became another item that had to be carried, along with the tools and weapons, the babies, the young children and the ornamental wear, when it was time to move.

As we saw on page 33, increase rites were practised faithfully in the belief that they ensured a continual reproduction of the necessary vegetable and animal foodstuffs.

Despite all possible efforts at conservation and preservation the task of finding enough food remained a daily chore. Although the meat of the native wildlife was their major source of food, the Aboriginal people, with their deep understanding of natural forces, resources and ecology, preserved perfect harmony. It is significant that in forty thousand years or more of the occupation of Australia very few animal species became extinct. And those that did — some very ancient giant species — were killed off by the immense climatic and environmental changes of their prehistoric era rather than by the hunters of the day. As a comparison, more than two hundred separate wildlife species have become extinct in the short period since white occupation in 1788. Can we not learn something from this?

TOOLS, WEAPONS AND UTENSILS

T raditional tools, weapons and utensils were designed and fashioned by individual members of the various Aboriginal groups as a matter of necessity. They were fashioned from natural products available in each particular area or those that could be obtained by barter, including timber, stone, bone, string (strips of animal hide or shredded bark) and other sundry objects.

Fig. 7.1   A camp scene with a bark shelter and wooden implements.

© Australian Museum. Photo: T. Dick. 7708.

81

The importance of trees

The density and type of tree that grew in each area governed many aspects of the lives of the local people. Timber was a natural commodity of great importance, and it was used in making many different utensils, tools and weapons. Trees, whether used in constructions such as those described below or in their natural form, provided the only form of shade and shelter other than caves available to the Aboriginal people in the traditional period. (Caves were seldom used as the members of most groups believed that they were inhabited by evil spirits.) Most parts of the trees — leaves, bark, seeds etc. — were used as raw material for something — medicine, food, shelter, firewood. Even the gum, the sticky sap found beneath the bark of many trees, provided a form of glue.

Medicine

Medicinal practices varied to some degree from group to group. Almost all of the more commonly used medications were based on bark, leaves, sap or roots. There was a vast number of tried medicines covering all ailments, a few examples of which are given below.

Wattle bark, soaked and boiled, was drunk as a cough syrup. Stringy bark strips were used as bandages to stop bleeding and give support. A decoction of quinine bark was used for bathing sore eyes and as an antiseptic. (A decoction is a preparation obtained by simmering the ingredient in a small amount of water.)

The leaves from pepper senna trees were infused in hot water to produce steam, which was inhaled to relieve congestion. (An infusion is the result of pouring boiling water on leaves, like making tea.) A decoction of crushed pine leaves was allowed to cool, then applied to rashes and insect bites. Gum leaves, bruised and warmed, were used as poultices for snake bites, boils and headaches.

The crystallised sap from ghost gums was boiled until dissolved, then used to bathe sores, cuts, burns or ulcers. This concentrated solution is still highly regarded. Eucalyptus gum was used to fill dental cavities and relieve pain.

A decoction from grevillea roots was used to ease diarrhoea. Milk thistle was eaten raw to relieve severe pain and induce sleep.

Food

Some trees (including wattle and kurrajong) provided seeds that could be ground into flour. Others provided crops of wild fruits, berries and nuts in season. Leaves were also useful (see page 83). Trees provided the shelter needed for the breeding of birds, some small animals and many insects, all of which ultimately became sources of food for the Aboriginal people.

Bark

The bark of trees was stripped off in large sheets to be used in the making of canoes, shields and shelters. It was used as a canvas for the artists of the day. Bark plates and platters — with the smooth side facing upwards — were used for serving and eating food. Many decorations and a type of string were also made from bark.

Burial connections

Trees were important in the burial procedures of traditional Aboriginal people. On Bathurst and Melville Islands, for instance, large tree trunks were painted and carved symbolically as part of the funeral ceremony.

The bodies of the dead were at times wrapped in bark shrouds and left on elevated branches. Alternatively, bodies (particularly those of the very young) were wrapped in bark and placed in hollow trees or logs.

Bark slabs decorated with the totem design of a deceased person were in most instances left as grave markers. Some selected trees, their bark having been removed, were carved symbolically to show respect for a certain elder or some other important group member, who had been buried close by.

Leaves

Eucalyptus leaves were at times used during cooking to flavour the meat. Sometimes, too, a hot tea-like drink was made by boiling various strongly flavoured leaves. All manner of dried leaves were used to thatch the walls and roofs of the various shelters.

The large pandanus leaves of northern Australia were woven into mats, skirts, baskets and sails. The leaves of the creek fig tree were used as sandpaper. The large, pliable sheaths of the north coast bangalow palms were used as water containers. They were called pikkies. Lerp and manna were gathered from the leaves — mainly the eucalypts — in summer and autumn.

Fires

Trees provided the all-important firewood on which the Aboriginal people relied so much as a source of warmth and as a means of cooking. Charcoal from fires was used by artists. Ash was used in art work, mixed with fat and used to prevent sunburn in babies and also used as a salving ointment for all wounds, including accidental burning.

Shelter and shade

Trees in their natural form provided shade — much needed in hot, dry areas — for traditional people. In addition, the trees of all areas provided building materials used in the construction of shelters. When necessary the groups built windbreaks around their campsite, consisting of fallen branches, leaves and bark. They were usually 1–1.5 metres high and about twenty to thirty metres around. A whole group of people could shelter, sitting or resting, behind them.

Fig. 7.2a   A bark shelter — usually about 1 metre high and 2 metres wide. Extremely large slats of bark were used in the construction.

Fig. 7.2b   A windbreak — usually about 1 metre high and several metres long. These were made out of branches, leaves and bark and were usually curved providing shelter for a family or even a whole clan.

Some huge trees, such as the big red river gums of New South Wales, were often carefully and deliberately burned out on one side. While not killing the tree, a large section could then be hollowed out. A tree prepared in this

84

manner provided a temporary but secure shelter for a single person or, in some cases, a whole family, during a severe rain or wind storm.

The most common type of shelter throughout all areas was the lean-to, which could be constructed very quickly. It consisted of slabs of bark and clusters of logs which were leant against and then attached securely to an existing tree trunk. This kind of a shelter was usually about 1.5 metres high.

Fig. 7.2c A rounded hut — usually about 1.5 metres high and 3 metres long. These were built from anchored branches, twigs and leaves.

Fig. 7.2d A sleeping platform by night, a shelter from the sun or rain during the day.

In some areas a more substantial oval framework of solid sticks was built. It became the basis of the walls and roof of a hut, which was then thatched with leaves and strips of bark. These constructions were usually about two metres high and two or three metres wide. They were used by families as a shelter from the elements, particularly at night. A fire at the entrance gave warmth in the cold weather and helped keep mosquitoes and flies away in the summer.

As there were several hundred different languages among the Aboriginal groups, there were many different names for these dwellings, such as *gunyah*, coming from the language of groups in New South Wales, *wurley* from South Australia and *mia mia* and *oompy* (from which has come *humpy*) used in Queensland.

Sometimes, if a large tree was blown down, the branches left protruding could be covered and a quickly made shelter would result. This was necessary if a storm came up suddenly.

In some campsite areas, particularly in hot or wet areas, sleeping platforms were constructed about a metre above the ground. Four tree trunks or four posts placed together were used as the base. A light timber framework was then built and attached to them. A second framework would then be attached about a metre above the first. This shelter was thatched, like the gunyahs, with leaves and bark and provided shelter from the rain and sun.

Fig. 7.2e   A special sleeping platform — large enough for two — built high over a gently smouldering fire.

The sleeping platforms were most useful because people sleeping on the lower framework were able to enjoy the breeze in the warm weather and were above the damp ground in the wet. In cold weather a low fire was lit under the framework for added warmth. In very cold weather the sides of this construction were filled in with bark so that even more protection was given.

Fig. 7.2f   A large rounded hut — usually about 1.5 metres high and up to 4 metres long. Sometimes clay was added to the walls and roof which made the hut more durable.

Fig. 7.3 An example of a shelter tree. The inside section was deliberately burnt out to provide a temporary, secure shelter from a severe rain or wind storm.

During the traditional period most shelters built were meant to be temporary, but some groups, particularly in the tropical regions, did construct semi-permanent dwellings. These were usually oval in shape and were larger than the gunyah/wurley styles. They consisted of a sturdy framework of sticks, which were set firmly into the ground. The walls and roof would be thatched with leaves, usually from the pandanus trees, and then covered with special clay, which created a mud hut effect.

Wooden weapons

Spears

During the traditional period of Aboriginal history spears were used as a hunting and, to a lesser extent, as a combat weapon by the men of all areas. Spears were the most common of all the wooden implements and there were a great many varieties. The simplest and most basic, which were used by all including the groups in Tasmania, were about two to three metres long. They were each sharpened to a point and hardened by fire.

The mainland groups fashioned many additional specimens that were more elaborate and incorporated ground pieces of stone, bone or shell as spearhead points. Mammal and fish teeth were also used for this purpose in most areas. Spearhead points were fastened to the wooden shaft by gum or strips of kangaroo hide. Spear shafts varied in length from one to three metres, depending on the task for which each one was made.

In areas close to water, a special type of spear was constructed for use in fishing. They were usually about two metres long and had three or four prongs. In some instances the prongs were carved from the same piece of timber as the shaft but occasionally honed pieces of bone were attached.

The men of all groups decorated their spear shafts with carvings and paintings which had totem significance to their group or were related to 'hunting magic' rituals. The most spectacular of all spears were those from the northern Australian areas.

Not only was the decorative patterning especially rich and rare in these areas but so too was the design of the weapon itself. Collections include spears that have double- and even triple-sided barbs. The double-sided spears, which were all expertly carved, usually contained eight to ten barbs, each about eight centimetres wide, on each side. Each of the barbs sloped backwards and was about ten centimetres long.

The triple-sided weapons, which often had up to eighteen small, sharp barbs on each side, were even more awesome in appearance. Each shaft was ornately patterned and often had tassles of ochre-dyed string attached. Some such spears were created to be ceremonial artefacts only, but most were created to be used with devastating effect as weapons. The influence of the Torres Strait Islanders, the New Guineans and the Macassans, who occasionally visited the north of Australia in traditional times, is evident in the construction of these particular implements.

Spear-throwers

Spear-throwers were a significant invention of the Aboriginal people and were not found anywhere else in the world.

The best known Aboriginal word for spear-thrower is *woomera*, which is commonly used in all areas today. A woomera, made of soft wood, acts as an extension of the thrower's arm and therefore helps to project the spear with greater force. (The woomera increased the range and speed but aim tended to become more difficult, so much practice was needed before it could be used with best effect.)

There were several variations in shape but each woomera was usually about a metre long and rounded. A small piece of bone or flaked stone would be bound to the timber at the opposite end to which it was held. The butt end of the spear rested here before being held aloft and then thrown. A woomera could be used as a utensil when not in use as a spear-thrower.

Boomerangs

Contrary to popular belief, returning boomerangs were not used extensively by the traditional people. They were in evidence only in eastern and

Fig. 7.4   The creation of the returning boomerang is an ingenious Aboriginal achievement believed to be unique to Australia.

© Australian Museum. Photo: T. Dick. 7779.

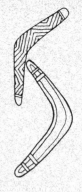

Western Australia and were not used at all until recent times in Central Australia, Tasmania or the Northern Territory.

The returning boomerangs were used most effectively in the areas around the Murray, Darling, Lachlan and Georges Rivers (the word *boomerang* comes from the Georges River area). One use was to startle birds and animals, driving them into a net which had been positioned in readiness.

They were used extensively in competitions between the men of each particular group and between neighbouring groups. At such times spectacular feats were performed not only in the length of the throw and the return but also in the many different manoeuvres which were attempted and mastered.

The creation of the returning boomerang is an ingenious achievement thought to be unique to Australia. It involves a complicated understanding of wind velocity and tip vortices. Helicopters function using the very same principle. (Helicopters were created from a patent secured by a recognised Aboriginal genius, David Unaipon, in the 1930s.)

The majority of traditional boomerangs, however, did not return. The non-returning varieties were called hunting boomerangs and were in reality specialised throwing sticks. Some of them had an edge that had been ground until it was sharp. Others had hooked ends and so were useful for tasks such as raking up coals when not being thrown.

The hunting boomerangs were made from the timber of one of the hardier species of wattle (neither eucalyptus nor pine timber was suitable). The hunting boomerangs were thought of as useful weapons, but the returning boomerangs, which were usually decorated very elaborately, were of course regarded as prized possessions. In some areas displays of boomerang throwing were given as part of sacred or special ceremonies. In all areas boomerangs were tapped together to reinforce the desired rhythm during corroboree dancing.

Clubs

The wooden club, which most hunters from all groups carried, is sometimes referred to today as a waddy or by an Aboriginal word, *nulla-nulla,* from the Wiradjuri language. Each club was formed from a single piece of timber. Most of them were about a metre long but varied greatly in shape from man to man and from area to area.

Some clubs were pointed, some double-ended, others were axe-shaped. Some had one end shaped like the head of a lizard or a bird. Most of them had decorated handles of some kind, usually depicting the totem of

Fig. 7.5   Returning from a successful hunt. The hunter
has caught a python. He would have used the shield as a
cover while stalking his prey.

© Australian Museum. Photo: T. Dick. 7719.

the maker. Each one revealed the carving skill and imagination of the man who had fashioned it. As a hunting or combat weapon they were invaluable. Seldom was a hunter seen without his club.

Shields

The men of all groups used shields as a protection in battle and as a cover while stalking their prey. Sheilds varied widely in shape and decoration. It seems that each group took pride in choosing a specific style, one that differed from others.

Most shields were fashioned from a single piece of timber, varying in shape. They were usually about thirty centimetres across the centre and about sixty centimetres long, tapering to a point at each end. The handle was usually stuck on or occasionally carved as part of the whole piece. The handle was usually in the centre. Mock shields were often made of bark and then highly decorated to be used in various rituals and ceremonies, including corroborees.

Wooden musical instruments

Didgeridoos

Didgeridoo is an Aboriginal word (originating in the Kimberley area) that refers to the wooden musical instrument used during corroborees and social dancing. A rhythmic droning sound — referred to today as *dreeing* — is created when the player blows into the hollowed section of the instrument in a certain manner. It was used mainly by the men of the Northern Territory and the Kimberley regions in the traditional period.

A didgeridoo was a hollow timber cylinder, averaging one to two metres in length. In the traditional period some were up to six metres long and several men were needed to carry them.

In traditional times the echoing rhythmic sound of a didgeridoo accompanied the chanting, clapping and stamping during a social corroboree or a serious ritual ceremony. Didgeridoos were usually decorated quite lavishly, usually with the totem of the maker or his group.

Didgeridoos are used effectively by both white and Aboriginal musicians today. The sound produced varies depending on the size and the method of blowing into the tube.

Bullroarers

Bullroarers were used during the traditional period by all groups. They were made of timber. These implements were known by different names in different areas. In contemporary times the European-given name *bullroarer* has been in common usage.

In the traditional period each bullroarer consisted of a flat piece of timber, suspended from a string, which was either a sliced strip of animal hide, a dried animal sinew or woven threads of bark. The base of a bullroarer could vary in diameter from fifteen centimetres to a metre, and each one was usually about a centimetre wide. Some were square, some round and some oval in shape. Bullroarers were usually painted with totem images and were usually highly decorated with feathers, strips of fur or fringes of string.

When in use, a bullroarer was swung forcibly above the user's head. When swung at arm's length, it made an eerie whirring sound, which became louder and more forceful as it was swung faster and faster. Its unusual sound gave a dramatic air to the most sacred ceremonies and celebrations. Some groups believed that the unusual sound of the bullroarer was the voice of the great Creator Spirit. Bullroarers were regarded as sacred in all areas and were used only by men. In some areas the women were never permitted to see them although they heard their exotic wail.

Tapsticks

Tapsticks and bark shakers of many varieties were used as percussion instruments by all Aboriginal people. They were used during corroborees, social dancing and by the children during play.

Wooden implements

Message sticks

A message stick was a type of passport that every traditional man carried if he had reason to leave his own area.

A message stick was a smallish piece of timber covered with incised marks of various kinds. It was a visible sign to the members of all other groups, no matter what their totem or language, that this traveller had good reason to be where he was.

Few Aborigines ever left their own area by choice, but some were sent to barter or trade with other groups or perhaps to arrange social events.

The message sticks were definitely necessary, for men found wandering in the wrong territory without authority were suspected of conjuring evil magic, planning to abduct the local women or commit some other crime. They were quite often punished severely, sometimes killed without question, if they were not carrying the required passport.

Digging sticks and spades

The women in all areas used digging sticks, which had been sharpened to a point and hardened at one end by fire. They varied in length and were used daily in their search for food.

Spades were also made and used in most areas. They were cleverly carved from the one piece of timber. The handles were about sixty centimetres long and three centimetres wide. The spade heads were quite deep with a sharpened edge.

Spades were used by the men to dig burrowing animals from their holes and to shovel hot coals and ashes. They were also needed for the digging of graves and in the elaborate bora ground preparation.

Wooden dishes

Any Aboriginal utensil made from timber is widely known today as a coolamon. The word *coolamon* comes from the Wiradjuri language and refers to watertight dishes of any size. Although at times coolamons were made from pliable bark, in most cases they were the skilfully hollowed out section of a suitable section of tree trunk.

Hours of work went into the making of them for, after the arduous hollowing-out process, the surface sections had to be smoothed to avoid splintering. Then some dishes — depending on their intended usage — were lavishly decorated with carving or painting.

Coolamons were used in many ways. Aboriginal women of all areas carried them as they collected yams, edible roots and seeds. Coolamons were also used to store or carry water — a most necessary task in the arid inland areas — and also to hold ochre. In addition, leftover meat and other food was stored in them, with bark lids being used when necessary.

Special coolamons longer and narrower than usual were used as portable cradles. Babies, wrapped in kangaroo-skin rugs, slept peacefully in them on the softness of sand. A coolamon cradle, being rounded at the base, could be gently rocked to and fro.

Tjuringa boards

A tjuringa board is an ancient, lengthy piece of trimmed timber or bark which is symbolically patterned. In the traditional period each one was regarded as sacred and was displayed only at ceremonies.

A tjuringa board was said to embody the spirit of a revered totem ancestor, and each one was accepted as having been created by the spirits in times long past. Like the individual tjuringa stones, each board was patterned to emulate the particular totem of the group responsible for its care.

The boards, being sacred, were kept out of sight except during ritual ceremonies. Even then they were seen only by a chosen few. They were passed down from generation to generation and were always regarded with awe and reverence in all areas. Many tjuringa boards still lie hidden.

Sticks

Sticks were used in the construction of shelters, rafts and some fish and animal traps. Sticks and twigs of an unusual shape were sought and used as part of individual body decoration, whenever a ceremony was approaching. Strong, straight sticks, sharpened to a point, were used as awls and prongs. Whenever kangaroo tail sinews were cut, or the hide sliced into strips, the resultant 'string' was wrapped around strong, straight sticks for later use. A brush for an artist could be made by hammering one end of a stick. Children found them useful for drawing picture stories in the sand or soil. Strong, straight sticks were used as splints for broken bones.

Aboriginal watercraft

During the thousands of years of Aboriginal occupation of Australia waterways were all important as major sources of food and water and, to a lesser extent, as recreational areas.

The craft of canoe-making was therefore also important. Down through the centuries, groups in different areas found that they had to adapt their skills to suit the raw materials available in their area. For example, the easy-to-work softwood timber of Queensland was not available in the west or south of Australia.

In the seventeenth and eighteenth centuries, many of the early European navigators reported seeing Aboriginal watercraft. Abel Tasman was probably the first. He reported seeing Aboriginal men using raft-like structures off the north-west coast in 1642.

However, canoes and other watercraft had most definitely been a significant part of the lives of these people for many thousands of years before this.

Rafts

Rafts were used in most areas close to waterways throughout Australia. There were several varieties. Often a single log was floated as a raft along the coast or downstream of the inland waterways. One or more people would sit on it or cling to it as it drifted.

Larger rafts were constructed of several thin branches, as well as strips of bark or reeds tied together. When five or six of these clusters were bound strongly together, a quite large platform was created on which six or eight people — a family — could ride.

Fig. 7.6   A raft on the beach.   © Australian Museum. Photo: T. Dick. 2193.

An even stronger and larger type of raft was also commonly used in most areas. It was constructed of several long, stout logs tightly bound together with strong bark cord or strips of kangaroo hide. Often a hut, consisting of reeds, bark and grass, was built on such a raft. At night a fire would be lit in the centre, established on a base of clay which was packed about ten centimetres thick and sixty to seventy centimetres long and wide. The fire provided light while the raft glided along in the dark shallow waters. It also gave warmth and, to some extent, protected the travellers from mosquitoes.

Rafts such as these were usually propelled by a strong person with a long pole, usually the reverse end of the fishing spear.

Dugout canoes

The dugout canoe is comparatively new to the Aboriginal people. The idea was introduced to the northern groups by various visitors — Macassan, Melanesian and Indonesian navigators. These visitors also introduced the outrigger with its square-shaped sail. Dugout canoes were made and used only in the northern areas of Australia because that was the only place where the necessary soft wood timber was available.

The most commonly used dugout was fashioned from the trunk of a tree which had been cut down and carefully hollowed out. Each such canoe took several men, working with their stone axes, chisels and adzes, several days to complete. When finished, the canoes were usually from two to six metres long and could carry several people. The dugouts were propelled by paddles and were used for fishing and for turtle and dugong hunting. They were never taken far out to sea because they were very unstable and often capsized, even though they were unsinkable.

More elaborate and even larger canoes were also built and used in northern Australia. Some could carry up to twenty occupants and were equipped with anchors made of stone. These larger canoes had ridged seats and sails woven from pandanus leaves. They looked quite sophisticated and were much more stable than the smaller ones. The construction of such a canoe took months of hard precise work from a team of eight or nine men. In calm weather the Aboriginal people could travel long distances in them and so were able to visit and barter with groups on the offshore islands.

The spectacular dugout canoes of Arnhem Land were more stable, although much smaller. Using strong, well-made paddles, the traditional fishermen of this area could keep their particular craft under control even in very heavy seas. These canoes were stable because they were made of hard wood. They were constructed from the timber of the huge paperbark trees in that area. Weeks of patient skilled labour went into hollowing out such wood. Consequently, the canoes were usually only large enough for one or two passengers. Similar canoes are being constructed and used effectively by the Aboriginal men of Arnhem Land today, although steel, not stone, axes are now used and outboard motors have been added.

Bark canoes

The traditional people in the southern coastal areas and the northern inland areas did not have the softwood timber needed for dugouts so they used

© Australian Museum. Photo: T. Dick. 7754.

Fig. 7.7 Men spearing fish from a bark canoe.

bark in the construction of their canoes. Different groups used different construction methods.

In north-western Queensland and the Northern Territory, the canoes were made of several long strips of bark tied together, usually with strong bark cord.

During this operation several forked branches, adjustable to varying heights, were used as ladders or platforms so that some men could work the high areas while others worked from ground level.

Before each massive sheet of bark was finally separated from the tree, a series of reed ropes was placed around it. This allowed the sheet to slip gently to the ground, thus preventing it from crashing heavily and splitting.

At this stage a small fire was lit and the sheet of bark was held over it. The heat rendered the bark more pliable and therefore easier to mould. When ready, the sheet was turned smooth side up. The ends were then chipped to a point, drawn tightly into shape and securely fastened, about forty centimetres from each end, with thin strips of kangaroo hide or sinew.

Clay was used at both ends to prevent water from entering. This type of canoe was propelled, like the rafts, by a long strong pole and so could only be used in shallow water. It was used mainly for fishing.

Much of the fishing was done at night, so a small fire was often lit on a clay base on the canoe. The fire gave the lone fisherman or woman light and warmth. Some bark canoes had a very sharp prow, which enabled them to cut their way through the thick water reeds that grew in abundance in some inland waterways.

After some months' use a canoe became waterlogged and so the manufacturing process would have to begin again.

Along the southern coast, the canoes were made from the bark of the eucalyptus trees. The bark had to be stripped off in one piece, then trimmed. Each chunk was usually about three to five metres long and one to two metres wide.

Along the inland river systems of New South Wales and Victoria the canoes were similarly constructed from the bark of the giant red river gums, which grew prolifically in this area. The red river gum bark was ideal as it was very thick and slightly curved. Bark from the mountain ash, several different species of box tree, blue gum and stringy bark was also used on occasion.

To obtain a single piece of bark large enough for a canoe, several skills had to be employed by as many as ten to twelve men, all working together.

Initially, the tree was carefully chosen. The condition of the sap (which decreed whether the bark would be too brittle), the tree size, its age and position would all be considered before the choice was made. The desired

Fig. 7.8   Canoe trees in Eugowra, N.S.W.

size and shape of the piece of bark to be cut would then be marked on the side of the tree with a stone axe. While two or three men were completing this task, others with hammer stones and the butt end of their stone axes, would tap and pound at the bark so as to loosen it.

When this was completed, other men would slowly insert wooden or stone wedges around the outline and skilfully and slowly begin to prise it away from the tree.

Canoe trees

A tree that has had sections of its bark stripped off for canoe-making is today referred to as a canoe tree. There are quite a number of these trees, some centuries old yet still living. One of the largest canoe trees ever found is on a Pastures Protection Reserve at Paytens Bridge, Eugowra, New South Wales. This giant red river gum stands on the banks of the Lachlan River, and the scar on the tree, about ten metres long and two metres wide, is still clearly visible. Several double canoe trees have also been found in this area, some of which can be seen from the Forbes-Eugowra Road.

Early settlers destroyed many canoe trees as they cleared their land for the plough, but hundreds can still be seen throughout central New South Wales and the Murray River area extending into South Australia. Their huge scars stand as a lasting tribute to the skill and ingenuity of the indigenous people of Australia.

Stone implements

Rocks and stones are a natural product that the traditional Aboriginal people used to the full in their widely scattered societies. Stone to suit the different needs of these people varied quite considerably, as did the types of stone available in each area.

To cater for the varied needs of scattered groups, elaborate trade routes throughout Australia were established. Some of them were maintained for thousands of years. Some stone implements have been found as far as two thousand kilometres away from the original quarry. The best known of the trading quarries are those at Lancefield and Mount William in Victoria and Mount Harris in New South Wales.

The Nepean River, near Castlereagh in New South Wales, was also a place where many stones — large river pebbles — were exchanged. The stones from this area were especially useful in making axes and chisels. The Blue Mountains area of New South Wales, with its massive sandstone deposits, was also particularly useful to the local Aborigines and to those who came to barter.

Throughout Australia, in recent times, traditional stone implements of many kinds have been found in huge numbers. They have been found around the original campsites, which were the lake shores, the river and creek banks, the claypan flats and any place where water was to be found, such as around the underground springs in hilly areas. Others have been found at random on various farming properties, brought to the surface by the plough.

A study of these implements reveals four major groups: ritual stones, tools, weapons and those with various other uses.

Ritual stones

Ritual stones from the traditional period are more rarely found today than any other Aboriginal stone implement. There are two major reasons for this. First, there never were very many in existence. Each group had only one collection, carefully guarded and passed down to each new generation. Second, during the traditional period most of the ritual stones were kept hidden in a secret, sacred place. The hiding place was known only by one or two specially chosen elders of each group, and these men guarded the secret most fervently.

During the traditional period of Aboriginal history — the nineteenth century — most of the established Aboriginal groups were forced to disband. In most instances the members were forcibly taken to a mission. In many instances the mission was far distant from their home area so the people chose to leave the ritual stones in their sacred secret place. Most still lie there, undiscovered, to this day. Those that have been collected are documented as follows.

Muraian stones

Muraian stones were ritual stones. They appear to be either natural river stones or rounded pieces of rock. They have been found in the Kimberleys and in Arnhem Land. Each was originally painted geometrically with designs of totemic significance. Most muraian stones appear to be very ancient. It is thought that in some way they represented the spiritual tie of each group with its totem ancestors. The Aboriginal people today who know of their usage have chosen to keep this knowledge sacred and secret.

Rainbow Serpent eggs

Rainbow Serpent eggs were in evidence during most of the ritual ceremonies of most groups throughout Australia. At other times they were carefully stored in a secret place. The stones were usually about the size of an emu's egg or slightly larger. They were accepted as being the eggs of the great Rainbow Serpent, which had, in the Dreaming, assisted in the creation of all areas of Australia.

Rainbow Serpent eggs were passed down from generation to generation for centuries in all areas and were regarded with awe. Their power was especially strong and relevant at initiation ceremonies. At such times, stories of the Rainbow Serpent's powerful influence and significance would be told to the young initiates.

Message stones

In scattered areas of South Australia a large number of flat, thin stone bars have been collected. Each one has a pattern of straight grooves carved into it. There appears to be no accurate record explaining their original purpose, but they are generally regarded by researchers as being a form of message stone; the message involved a ritual practice and was intended for a totem ancestor.

Cyclon

Cyclons are known in some archaeological journals as cylindro-conical stones. Each one is cylindrical in shape with a convex butt about seven centimetres wide and twenty to thirty centimetres long. This stone tapers to the opposite end which is pointed and rounded.

The stones in contemporary collections are made of soft argillaceous rock or sandstone, quartzite, basalt or phyllite, with a few of baked clay. Each cyclon has either a plain or an incised surface on which various motifs are carved. These motifs resemble kangaroo tracks, emu tracks, or herringbone, straight or rounded lines. It appears that these stones were commonly used in the Darling River area, near Wilcannia and around the old lake shore in western New South Wales. Some have also been found in central New South Wales.

It is known that cyclons were used in ritual ceremonies for hundreds of years, but their exact purpose remains secret except perhaps to a few initiated Aboriginal people from the areas mentioned.

Tjuringa stones

The use of personal tjuringa stones during the traditional period was apparent right throughout Australia, but more original specimens have been discovered in Central Australia than anywhere else. More is known about them than about the cyclon or the message stones.

Each of those collected was made from a flat slab of micaceous stone, that is, quartz which contained glimmering specs of aluminium silicate.

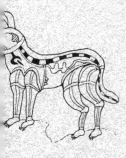

These were trimmed at the edges and ground to a pear shape. Each one was originally painted all over with red ochre or fat and charcoal. Traced on to this coloured surface was a design of half or full concentric circles together with imitation animal tracks.

The designs varied according to the particular totem of the group or the person. Those in existence today range in size from three to seventy-six centimetres long and from twenty-seven millimetres to three centimetres thick. Each has an individual decorative design.

Each tjuringa stone was said to embody the spirit of an ever-present and protective totem ancestor. A tjuringa stone was carried by each person or left close by. They were essential in the private and spiritual life of each individual and were particularly precious. In most areas the tjuringa stone (or stones) belonging to a deceased person was buried with that person.

Legendary stones

Stones classified as legendary stones or rocks had the natural shape of an animal, the moon or the features of some aspect of a legend with a sacred origin.

Legendary stones ranged in size from small water-washed pebbles, which represented eggs or a section of a particular animal, to huge boulders set in a hillside. Each one reminded the members of the group of some particular legend from the Dreaming lore or perhaps a prophecy for the future.

Such stones were secretly stored, unless too large, and incorporated in various ways in initiations and burials and other significant ceremonies. Some of the existent traditional art is done on legendary rocks and in sacred caves and crevices.

Marker stones

Groups of marker stones have been found in many areas of Australia. The stones collected are of no specific type or size. When found they were stacked in piles to mark a significant sacred spot. Others were found stacked in rows to mark paths that led to sacred ceremonial grounds. Unfortunately, modern cultivation has destroyed or disarranged many of the original and ancient piles.

Magic stones

A variety of magic stones (named and catalogued by twentieth-century non-Aboriginal people) were used in the ceremonies of all Aboriginal groups throughout Australia. They were used by the elders, usually by one designated head man.

Magic stones of many kinds were used in the process of evoking the special power needed for rain-making, contact with the spirits, the curing and the causing of sickness (as a punishment) and to create propitious hunting conditions. Magic stones usually comprised rock crystals, such as quartz, calcite or gypsum. When not in use they were stored carefully and in a secret place. Many still lie hidden.

Stone tools

Stone was used prolifically in all areas in the construction of tools and weapons. Because of their weight stone tools were made and left at various places along each campsite circuit, which saved having to carry them continually from one place to another.

Millstones

Millstones are sometimes known as grinders. They are the largest of the stone implements used during the traditional period. Some have been found which are fifty centimetres wide, six centimetres thick and a metre long, the edges being trimmed to an egg shape.

Millstones were usually made from a quarried slab of sandstone. They were made and used in all areas but have been found mainly in western New South Wales.

Women used the millstones to grind the seeds which they had collected from the wattle and kurrajong trees as well as the various spinifex grasses. The women made dampers from the flour they produced. The men used the back or side of these large implements to sharpen their axes and chisels.

Percussion stones

Percussion stones, in modern classifications, have been aptly named hammer stones and anvil stones. Their names fit their uses.

The hammer stone was probably the first real human tool. It was a most important and versatile tool for all early civilisations, including the Aboriginal people.

The hammer stones were usually made from river stones and varied greatly in size depending on the user's needs. Hammer stones were used for the knapping, trimming, breaking and pounding of other stones, bones, seeds and shells and also for shredding bark.

Fig. 7.9 The hammer stone was an important and versatile tool for all early civilisations. These people are using them to make new implements.

© Australian Museum. Photo: T. Dick. 7765.

The anvil stones were usually flat stones, round or egg-shaped, which measured about thirty centimetres across and were no more than six centimetres thick. In the centre an area was painstakingly chiselled out and roughened so that it would hold an object firmly while the craftsman further shaped it with a hammer stone. Axes were fashioned in this way.

Whetstones

Whetstones are in fact small millstones. These stones are a type of portable implement that was common in the traditional period in inland New South Wales, but apparently rare in other areas. They were either round or oval in shape, ranging from five to twenty-five centimetres in length and one to two centimetres in width. Some had a grinding surface on both ends.

Chisels

Chisels were virtually a type of axe head, the difference being that they were much longer. They usually had a smaller cutting edge than the axes. Some chisels were affixed by gum to a short handle, and some were tied to their handles with strips of kangaroo hide. They were used like axes to pry the

bark from trees and to split timber. They were also used by the women as they dug in the soil for yams and witchetty grubs.

Blades

Many of the stone implements which have been grouped together under the heading of 'blades' are at times classified individually as knives, oblique trimmed blades (which had a second cutting edge) and bondi points or scrapers. They have been classified separately to show slight variations from the norm. Examples of each from the traditional period have been found in several areas.

Each one shows a high degree of craftsmanship, which involved grinding, flaking and pecking of the highest order. They were made mainly from chert or quartzite rock. When finished they were used as spearheads or as a cutting implement held in the hand. Some had a very sharp edge which was needed for carving, engraving or cutting animal hides into strips.

Stone weapons

Stone weapons from the traditional period varied in type and usage, and many original specimens exist today.

Stone axes

Stone axes were among the most prolifically used stone weapons. They were used by all groups, and many different styles, designs and sizes were originally created.

Most of the myriad axes held in collections today are large uniface stones with a single cutting edge which have several chinks flaked or chipped into one side. Some of the chinks provide a hand grip, while others provide secondary trimming that gives a second cutting edge if needed. Uniface axes vary greatly in size and shape but overall the cutting edge of those that were knapped or flaked is greater, although much less precise than the ground-edged axes, which were also used by all mainland groups.

The ground-edged axes were made from river stones — the especially 'hard' types. Some of these were systematically ground to a point at one end, while the cutting edge of others was obtained through a combination of grinding, flaking and pecking. (The Tasmanian groups do not appear to have used the technique of grinding.)

Up to five hundred hours could go into the making of one such axe, for the grinding of stone was a very slow process. Stone axes of many styles were used to cut and carve timber, to cut and trim chunks of bark and, if needed, as a weapon in battle.

Fig. 7.10   Using a chisel to remove bark from a tree for shield-making.   © Australian Museum. Photo: T. Dick. 7788.

The ground-edged axes in contemporary collections range in size from two centimetres wide and five centimetres long to about eight centimetres wide and twenty centimetres long. Hafted axes — those with a handle — were common in most areas, but along the Lachlan River, New South Wales, and in some other areas the axes were hand-held.

Left-handed axes, double-ended axes and axe heads hafted on one side are among those that have been collected. These variations show clearly how some traditional craftsmen varied the norm to suit their particular needs.

Fine stone points

Many small uniface points of stone have been discovered. Each one has been skilfully made for a special purpose. Some of them, it seems, were originally mounted in gum at the end of a spear to form the spearhead. Others were mounted on the sides of a spear shaft in rows which pointed backwards, and acted as barbs. Some stones have exceptionally fine-pointed microlithic edges. It is not known how such microscopically cut edges were achieved in the traditional era.

The Bogan pick

There are few Bogan picks in existence today. Sometimes they are classified as cyclons. It would seem this type of pick was used in the traditional period in the same areas as the cyclon. The name probably originated from the Bogan River, New South Wales, where record of the first one discovered by whites was made.

The body of each was pecked extensively with a slight polish over it on some specimens. Those still in existence range in size from fifteen to thirty-five centimetres long and five to eight centimetres wide. The base of each was flaked off to create a rough flat surface, which had a full circle groove about a third of the distance from the base.

We can find no accurate account of their original purpose. The stones that have been collected appear to be very ancient. They could have been used to deliver a series of quick blows to the centre of the forehead and so steady or stun a beast long enough to spear it. It is also thought that they were used as part of hunting rituals, possibly as implements of magic designed to mesmerise the huge and now extinct prehistoric creatures such as the diprotodon.

The diprotodon, a creature somewhat like a giant wombat which walked on all fours, lived in Australia in Pleistocene times. It is accepted as being the largest known marsupial and it stood about two metres high and three to four metres long. Its head was huge and was supported by an exceptionally thick neck. It was a plant-eating creature. In 1892 a veritable graveyard of diprotodon bones was found in the dried-up bed of Lake Collabonna, South Australia. Earlier remains had been found at Wellington, New South Wales. The diprotodon roamed Australia twenty thousand years ago together with a close relative, the nototherium, and giant kangaroos, which stood up to three metres tall.

Other uses of stone

Shelves built of rocks and stones were used in fire areas as an aid to cooking. Large circular-shaped walls of compacted stone were built in waterways, as fish traps. Stone weights held fishing nets in place. Nose pins and death pointers were occasionally fashioned from stone (most were bone).

The aoyurka

Although rare, several aoyurka stones have been collected and catalogued. They are all T– or Y– shaped and roughly flat. They are usually polished and are either pecked or flaked. The examples collected to date have come from the Cairns and Innisfail districts. Very little is recorded about their original usage.

Throwing stones

In all areas stones were used to stun or panic animals in an effort to drive them into a net or some other trap. The throwing of stones was also, in most areas, one of many competitive sports. Some of the stones used were naturally round in shape, while others were chipped or ground into the desired shape. Some had grips for the thumb and index finger pecked or flaked into them.

Other sports involved pieces of sandstone or clay fashioned into a ball-shaped object or a circular disc. These were spun on hard, level ground or a flat rock surface.

Fish hooks

Pieces of stone were utilised as fish hooks in many areas, particularly in the northern areas. The stones were tied to the end of the line.

Ornaments

Small stones were often used with other materials to create decorative headgear and necklaces. In most instances these were painted vividly.

Stone utensils

Small portable rocks with a natural or hand-made concave section were always useful as containers. They were used to hold water. Other uses included storing ochre for artists or leftover foods.

Covers and caverns

Round flat pieces of granite about forty centimetres across and about six centimetres thick were often trimmed and used to cover the naturally concave sections of some boulders. If no natural recesses could be found, a hole up to fifty centimetres deep was at times laboriously hollowed out. These stone caverns were used for water storage, with the cover preventing evaporation or pollution from the wind.

Toys

Spinning tops and dolls of all sizes and shapes were sculpted from stone for children.

Fig. 7.11 It took many hours to flake, chip and grind as stone implements of many kinds were created. Children watch and learn.

© Australian Museum. Photo: T. Dick. 774

112

Other materials

One of the most significant features in the lifestyle of the traditional Aboriginal people was their ability to utilise all of nature's offerings to the full. Shells of all sizes were used as utensils, decorations and playthings. In addition to timber and stone, they also used bone, other animal materials such as teeth and skins, and string, made in various ways.

Bone

Bone was an important raw material and was used extensively in the making of tools and ceremonial ornaments. Bone was readily available but had to be fashioned while fresh or it would become brittle and break.

The most significant men and women of various groups in the northern areas wore nose bones. These bones were pointed at both ends and were usually polished. They ranged in length from five to twenty centimetres. The positioning of the nose bone was often part of a special ceremony, proclaiming the rise in status of that particular person.

The rib and the leg bones of some birds and mammals were fashioned into awls. Awls in the traditional period varied from five to thirty centimetres long. Usually the joint was left on one end and the other was ground to a point on an abrasive stone.

The larger awls were used to scrape and gouge. The smaller awls were used to peg the animal skins out to dry and to perforate the edges of those hides which were to be sewn or bound together.

Mudak is the Aboriginal name given to the short spear-like weapon which had a sharpened bone as its point. In the traditional era, the point was set with gum or bound to its wooden handle with kangaroo sinew or tendon. It was used mainly for fishing in shallow water, coastal or inland.

Many different bones — particularly animal and shark teeth — were used as decorations. Some were brightly painted before being threaded to make a necklace or an armlet.

Bone knives were used in all areas in the traditional period, and many of these are still in existence today. They were made from the rib bones of larger animals and the edges were ground until they became sharp. Sometimes the shoulder blades were taken from the carcass of a kangaroo or wallaby and then sharpened for use in this way.

Bone knives were useful for slicing cooked meat or cutting of hides into strips.

Bone needles with an eye were fashioned and used in traditional times in some areas of New South Wales and Victoria. They were used with string to stitch animal skins together in the making of cloaks and rugs.

The werpoo was a type of dagger used by traditional groups in northern Queensland. It was a feared implement, designed and used to kill.

Fashioned from a curved emu bone, it was tapered from the joint at one end. The length varied up to thirty-six centimetres. When used, it was thrust though the victim's rib cage and into the heart.

The bone implement best known to most people today is the death pointer, often referred to as 'the bone'. The pointer was kept hidden and used in all areas as an extreme punishment. Although used sparingly, it was feared by all. It was believed without question that powers of deadly evil hidden within the bone were projected into the body of anyone at whom it was pointed. There was no escaping its awesome power; to have the bone pointed at one was a definite death sentence.

A death pointer was usually made from the leg bone of a kangaroo or an emu, but in a few groups a human leg bone was used. In the making one end was ground to a sharp point while the other was usually left attached to the original joint. The entire bone was then covered in a sticky gum substance from which was hung a fringe of human hair as well as other decorations and sometimes also a smaller bone pointer. Death pointers ranged from ten to thirty centimetres in length.

The elders decided between them whether the bone should be used. One elder was then chosen to perform the ritual. The rhythmic chanting of a ritual song always accompanied the pointing of the bone. Without fail each victim died within a few days.

Other animal materials

Echidna (spiny anteater) spikes were used in most areas to puncture holes in the sections of animal hide which were to be sewn. They were also used to remove splinters and thorns, in engraving work and to make necklaces.

Animal hides were used in the making of cloaks, which were worn with the fur inside. Rugs of fur were also used in most areas and babies were often wrapped in or placed on a fur-lined skin. Some water-holders were made of skin. Strips of skin were sometimes used as a type of string. Strips of fur were used extensively as armbands, loin cloths and as a decoration.

The claws and beaks of eagles and other birds were used as engraving instruments and as decorations.

The teeth of some animals, mainly dingoes, wallabies, possums and kangaroos, were put to use as scrapers. To make a scraper several teeth or even the whole jaw bone from the animal would be set with gum into prepared wooden grooves. Once completed this scraping implement became a formidable weapon if need be and was capable of inflicting very serious wounds. Along the coastal areas, the teeth of whales, sharks, dugongs and other sea creatures were also used like this. Teeth were painted and used as decorations as well.

Feathers from the many brightly coloured native birds were used in all

Fig. 7.12 Dilly bags from Queensland. Dilly bags were made of string created from human hair, grasses, fibrous bark or sometimes from tendons and sinews from animal carcasses.

areas as decorations. Emu feathers were used in the making of kurdaitja shoes, which were worn by chosen elders on special occasions. Other natural materials used for ornamentation, particularly during ceremonies, included twigs, dingo tail tassles, nuts, wild flowers and berries of various kinds. No doubt there were many more.

String

String was used prolifically by the people of all groups in all areas during the traditional period of Aboriginal history. It was created in several different

115

ways, sometimes from human hair, many strands of which were interwoven; sometimes from long-stemmed grasses or from fibrous bark; sometimes tendons and sinews taken from an animal carcass were used. At times animal hides were cut into thin strips and dried, then used as string.

The Aboriginal people used the string they created in many different ways. The women of all groups made small carry bags — often referred to as dilly bags — which were held in the hand or hung over the shoulder. Sometimes leaves were cleverly woven into the framework. The women also made larger, stronger bags in which babies and young children could be carried, positioned on their mother's back.

The men plaited string of different kinds to make a strong rope which assisted them when climbing high trees. String was used to bind or stitch together (depending on the area) possum or kangaroo skins to make cloaks, rugs and water carriers. String was used to make many different toys, particularly for cats-in-the-cradle games, and as a decoration, when it would be coloured with ochre.

In all areas fishing nets of various styles were fashioned from string. Some of these were massive constructions that took several people many months to complete. It also took several people to position the finished nets correctly. Large nets were also made to snare land animals. Some nets were large enough to hold several animals at once so they were necessarily very strong as well.

A focus

on transitional

history

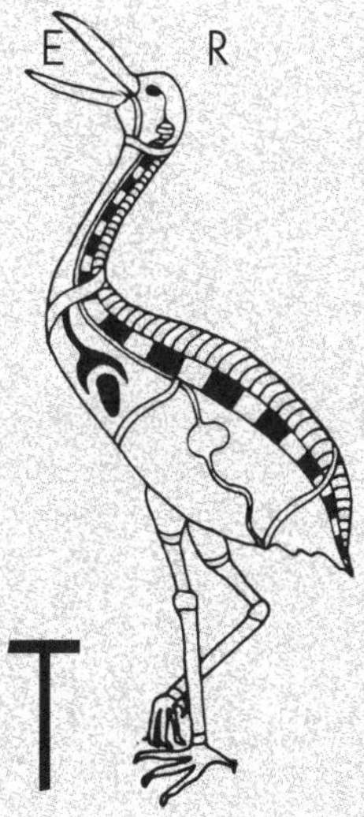

EARLY CONTACT

White people meet traditional Aborigines

Many ships were wrecked off various sections of the coast of Australia from the sevententh to the nineteenth centuries. Accounts of these wrecks reveal that some of the survivors were cared for by various Aboriginal groups.

It is well known also that, after the British penal colony had been formed in the late eighteenth century, many convicts from all areas managed to escape into the surrounding bushland. Many escapees were helped and given refuge by the Aboriginal people. The accounts of a few of these early liaisons give an insight into the personality of the traditional people as well as the history of this land.

Fig. 8.1 Breastplates were usually worn on a chain of some sort. The Wolgal people, of which Murray Jack was said to be "King" are from the south-east of N.S.W.

Mitchell Library, State Library of N.S.W.

The Batavia incident

At dawn on 4 June 1629 a Dutch merchant ship called *Batavia* ran aground in the Wallabi Island group, about seventy-five kilometres from present-day Geraldton in Western Australia. Most of the passengers, including men, women and children, were saved and quickly settled on three separate islands under the control of a man called Jerome Cornelius.

The captain, Francis Pelsaert, set sail in a small boat for the island of Java where he hoped to obtain help for those he had left behind. While he was absent, however, Jerome Cornelius persuaded several of his henchmen to murder all the survivors on the first island. When this was done they then attempted to murder those on the adjacent island, but some of these people managed to escape to the third island, where a man called Webbye Hayes took charge.

Cornelius and his men planned to murder every one of the survivors so that they could seize the rescue ship when it arrived and then escape with it and the treasure from the shipwrecked *Batavia*. Webbye Hayes, the people on his island and those who had survived the previous massacre were in battle with the treacherous Cornelius and his men when Captain Pelsaert returned. (The governor of Java had meanwhile lent him a yacht with which to rescue the castaways.) The mutineers were quickly defeated and captured. They were subsequently tried for mutiny and murder, then hanged from gallows erected on Seal Island. (These were the first recorded European executions on Australian soil.)

Two of the mutineers who had not been involved in the killings were spared, but were later marooned on the mainland of Australia as a punishment. They were instructed to discover whatever they could about the new land and report back to Dutch ships that visited in the future. These two men were the first Europeans to live for any length of time in Australia. They failed to report to any future ship, possibly because they did not wish to return to white society and further condemnation.

It is accepted that they lived with the Aboriginal people and became assimilated into their society. Several light-skinned Aborigines were later seen in that area and were thought to be their descendants.

John Tarwood and John Watson

John Tarwood and John Watson lived for about five years with the Aboriginal group based near Port Stephens, New South Wales, during the years 1794 to 1799.

Both men were convicts who had been transported to Sydney for life. The two had escaped with a third convict, shortly after their arrival. The third escapee had died soon afterwards, and Tarwood and Watson had then

headed for Tahiti in a stolen boat. The boat was eventually wrecked near Port Stephens where they were rescued and protected by the local Aboriginal people. The two men subsequently became totally involved with the traditional life of these people. When the crew of the ship HMS *Providence* discovered them five years later, each one had a wife and children.

Neither man at first wished to leave but eventually they were both persuaded to return to white society where they were both granted a pardon. It is not recorded whether they contacted their Aboriginal families again. They had both learned to speak the language of that group, so were able to work as interpreters during the years that followed.

They were the first to convince the authorities that the Aboriginal people spoke more than one language. There were actually five hundred languages, perhaps more, in existence throughout Australia at this time.

Thomas Pamphlett

Surveyor General John Oxley visited Moreton Bay in the ship HMS *Mermaid* in 1823. He was amazed when suddenly a man who appeared to be Aboriginal approached him and spoke to him in perfect English. The man was an English adventurer named Thomas Pamphlett.

Pamphlett, with three other men, had set off a year earlier to collect cedar from the islands off the coast of Sydney. Their small boat had been caught in a gale and swept off course. One of the men had died of thirst after twenty-one days without water, but Thomas Pamphlett and the two others survived and later lived with the Aborigines in that area.

Pamphlett and one of the other men returned with Oxley to Sydney. Twelve months later the third man was picked up by another vessel and returned. On their return each man spoke at great length of the culture and sound family structure of the Aboriginal people. In addition, they were able to give helpful geographic accounts of the area.

John Baker

John Baker was a convict who escaped from the Moreton Bay prison settlement in 1835. A group of Aboriginal people found him unconscious and near death from starvation and subsequently saved his life.

An Aboriginal woman claimed that he was her reincarnated son, Booralsha, who had died earlier. John Baker continued to be known by that name and lived with these people for fifteen years, adopting their ways and learning their language.

In 1840 he finally walked into the nearest settlement and gave himself up. The astonished officials there had believed him dead. Back in white society he gave valuable service as an interpreter and fought for the rights of the Aboriginal group who had befriended him. Because of this man, a fairly comprehensive record of the language spoken by the group in the upper Brisbane River area was made. This record has been retained to this day.

Barbara Crawford

Barbara Crawford came to Australia from Scotland in the 1840s. At the age of sixteen she left Sydney with a man named Thompson. He owned the ship *America,* and in it the two set out to salvage oil from a whaling ship which had been wrecked on Brampton Shoal, years earlier. When Thompson called at Moreton Bay, he was asked by the explorer Ludwig Leichhardt to join his impending overland expedition.

Thompson declined but promised when he reached Port Essington to help organise a party to be sent to meet the explorers. He was not able to keep this promise, however, as his ship, driven by a gale, was wrecked on the Queensland reefs soon after leaving Brisbane. He and all of his crew were either drowned in the wreck or while trying to swim ashore.

Barbara Crawford, who had married the captain during the journey, was rescued from the wreck by members of the Muralug Aboriginal group who ferried her back to shore in one of their canoes. She subsequently lived with these people for nearly five years.

In 1848 she returned to Sydney in HMS *Rattlesnake,* having been sighted and picked up at Evans Bay. She had been accidentally burned during the time she had been with the Aboriginal people. (Many suffered severe burning because they tended to sleep too close to the fire on very cold nights.)

Her return to her parents was dramatic, emotional and much discussed at the time. Although unable to read or write English, Mrs. Thompson was able to give the interested authorities much information about the Aboriginal way of life as well as hundreds of words from the language spoken in that area.

Jimmy Murrell

Jimmy Murrell was born in Essex in England in 1824. He was aboard a ship, *Peruvian,* which was wrecked off the Queensland coast in 1846. He was one of seven survivors who spent forty-two days on a raft, before coming at last to shore near Cape Cleveland.

Three of the seven died soon afterwards. The Aboriginal people who found the remaining survivors tended their wounds and gave them food. Despite this attention, a boy and two other men also died.

Jimmy Murrell was then the sole survivor. He remained with these people for several months. He later married an Aboriginal girl from a group near Port Denison. He became a trusted member of this group and lived with them for seventeen years. Although he lived harmoniously with them, they were aware that he wanted to return to his own people. A group of hunters on sighting a ship once tried to tell those on board about their white guest. Their kindly motives were misunderstood, and one of them was shot.

On another occasion, Jimmy Murrell himself came upon a shepherd's hut but, despite his attempts at friendly communication, the shepherd endeavoured to shoot him. As white settlement gradually spread closer, however, he was finally able to make contact. Once this was done, he decided, in 1863, to return and live again in the white way.

He reported later that his Aboriginal wife and others of the group had been very distressed as he prepared to leave them. 'It was a strangely touching scene,' he reported. 'There was a sharp struggle between the love I felt for these people and my own desire to live my "old" life. It almost broke my heart.'

He later settled in Bowen where he married a white woman and had a son. (It is not recorded whether any Aboriginal children had been born to him.) He did not forget the Aboriginal people, however, and is reported to have revisited them often. He worked untiringly in the next few years to ensure that they were able to remain undisturbed in the lower swampy area along the coast where for centuries their ancestors had lived. He himself did not live long after leaving them in 1863. He died two years later.

Before he died he tried unsuccessfully to persuade the authorities to send an expedition to search for the explorer Leichhardt, whose entire party had been lost in the interior for the past seventeen years. Murrell believed that some surviving members could be living with Aboriginal groups as he himself had. Many people agreed with him but nothing was ever done. It was later discovered that a Scot called William Stewart, a former runaway convict who had become a member of Leichhardt's party, did in fact live for nineteen years with Aboriginal people.

William Buckley

In 1835 a party of men led by the co-founder of Melbourne, John Batman, was astounded when they saw an unusual-looking light-skinned man among the Aborigines at Indented Head, Port Phillip. He stood more than two metres tall, had long shaggy fair hair and a beard that reached to his waist.

The man was William Buckley. During his early years in England he had been a bricklayer and a soldier before being transported to Australia in

1798 for theft. He escaped in 1803 with several others from the harsh convict settlement and sought the shelter of the bush. Very soon after, the escapees had encountered a group of Aboriginal men and a battle followed, resulting in the death of all the convicts except Buckley. He was spared because they thought he could have been the reincarnation of Murrungurk, a very tall member of their group who had recently died. He subsequently spent thirty-two years with these people.

He seemed physically fit when Batman returned him to white society, but was unable to act as an intermediary for he found it difficult to relearn English. In addition, he did not adjust well to the change of lifestyle. He was granted a pardon by the governor, but appeared fretful and discontented and did not live long after his return.

Narcisse Pellatier

Narcisse Pierre Pellatier, a French cabin boy, was the sole survivor of a ship wrecked on Rossel Island in 1858. He was found and cared for by a group of Cape York Aborigines and lived happily with them for seventeen years.

He literally grew from boyhood to manhood while with them. In 1875 he was taken against his will by well-meaning rescuers back to Somerset in England. He was unhappy there and tried to escape but was prevented and on this occasion sent back to France.

Years later Pellatier made his way back to Australia and spent the rest of his life with the Aboriginal group who had earlier befriended him.

Beeleechee

In the 1890s a police party, led by Inspector Lodge from Derby in Western Australia, brought in a group of young Aboriginal men whom they intended to question about the killing of a Chinese cook and a white stockman near Mount Hopeless. They were surprised to discover a light-skinned young man called Beeleechee among them. Although he was obviously European with blue eyes and very fair hair, he had the same initiation markings as the others and, surprisingly, could not speak or understand a word of English. The police were told that he had been found as a baby and reared by one of the Aboriginal women as her own.

Shortly after this, the historic first message was sent over the newly erected Kimberley to Perth telegraph line. The policeman who sent this message surprised all by stating that he had recently seen and talked with a white woman who had been living with the Aboriginal people there for more than twenty years.

The policeman said that she had told him in perfect English that she and her son were the only survivors of a ship which had been wrecked off

King Sound in the late 1860s. She said she was in good health and that they had both been well cared for.

Governor Broome, who received the message on the telegraph, invited the woman to return to what he called 'civilised' living. She declined his offer, again stating that she and her son were content and happy where they were. She asked nothing for herself but suggested blankets and flour would be appreciated by the others. Governor Broome sent a good supply of both and some tea.

In the years that followed, a young white man was repeatedly seen with these people, but the woman was never heard from again. It is not known whether Beeleechee was the son she spoke of or yet another white child who had been afforded the protection of these people.

Eliza Fraser

Captain James Fraser and his wife Eliza left Sydney on board the ship *Stirling Castle* in 1836. Six days from Sydney the ship struck a reef and suddenly went down.

Most of those on board, including the Frasers, then began a hazardous journey to safety in lifeboats. After a few days, while still stranded in the lifeboats Eliza Fraser gave birth to a baby who died soon afterwards. Three weeks later they landed on one of the Bunker Islands where several of the survivors stole the lifeboat and deserted the group.

The remaining castaways managed to reach Sandy Island which was later renamed Fraser Island. A party of the men set off from there, hoping to reach Brisbane and return to rescue the others. While they were gone some local Aboriginal men ferried the ailing captain, his wife Eliza and the other few survivors to the mainland in their canoes. Captain Fraser and the first mate died soon after reaching the mainland but the others survived and lived on with the Aboriginal people.

About three months later, three of the men who had set out earlier finally managed to reach Brisbane. An expedition led by John Graham was immediately sent in search of the others and soon located two cabin boys who had been living with a local Aboriginal group. Two days later they picked up the second mate, and several days later they located Mrs Fraser with yet another group. She appeared to be mentally disturbed. Distraught with despair and grief over the loss of her baby and her husband, Mrs Fraser did not appear to have adapted well to living with the Aboriginal people but was physically quite fit.

The Aboriginal people had regarded her as 'strange' yet would not release her until John Graham, who was later praised for his bravery, went through a special ritualistic procedure. It involved walking unarmed and unclad through two lines of Aboriginal men to collect her. This he did. The reason for this ritual was never explained, but the Aboriginal elders honoured their agreement. Mrs Fraser returned to England where she later married the captain of the ship on which she had returned.

There were hundreds of convicts other than those briefly mentioned in these accounts who managed to escape and elude recapture during this eventful and dramatic period of Australian history. In addition there were many explorers and adventurers who were listed as 'lost' during this era. It is most probable that most of these men — both the free and the bond — found a new life with the Aboriginal people and chose not to return to white society. The stories of each, were they known, would make interesting reading indeed.

Aborigines meet the first colonists

These brief accounts from the first years of white settlement detail the involvement of many Aboriginal people in the lives of the colonists. They reveal that in some instances at least there were definite, although misguided, attempts to forge a peaceful liaison.

Bennelong

In 1795 Governor Phillip, who had recently founded the New South Wales penal colony, made a special point of befriending two of the local

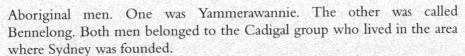

Aboriginal men. One was Yammerawannie. The other was called Bennelong. Both men belonged to the Cadigal group who lived in the area where Sydney was founded.

Governor Phillip encouraged the two to learn the ways of the white world. They learned pidgeon English quickly and appeared at first to enjoy the attention given them. Eventually they were taken to England.

Governor Phillip intended to have them explain some of their Aboriginal culture and so assist the English authorities to draw up sensible guidelines for the running of this new, mixed-race colony. At the time much was made of the experiment in the English and Australian press. It seemed that both men were received as honoured guests, both in the homes of the English officials and at the Houses of Parliament in London. In reality, however, they were treated as curiosities, and both men soon realised it.

Within a couple of months Yammerawannie, pining badly for his homeland, contracted pneumonia and died. Bennelong, also dispirited, was returned to Australia shortly afterwards.

This experiment aroused a great deal of interest at the time, but cannot be said to have been very beneficial, particularly for the black men. Bennelong, back in Sydney, continued to help with liaison, but the forced change in his lifestyle as well as an introduction to alcohol proved too traumatic for him. He remained friendly with the white men with whom he had associated, but gradually he became a pathetic figure unsure of himself in either society.

Had Europeans not come to these shores, Bennelong would have become a respected elder within his group and lived out his days in a secure, purposeful manner. As it was, his own people ultimately shunned him, and he died in 1813 in a bitter, drunken brawl. Bennelong Point in Sydney was named after him.

Bungaree

Bungaree was another Aborigine who became well known to the white population in the early nineteenth century. Bungaree had a vibrant, outgoing personality. He became a most helpful member of His Majesty's Navy and was a notable figure in Sydney society for more than thirty years.

In 1801 he and another young Aboriginal man named Nanbaree sailed with Matthew Flinders around Australia. The two of them became the first Aborigines to circumnavigate Australia. Later Bungaree was asked to do the trip a second time, which he did. He remained employed by the Navy until his death and was well respected by all, including each successive governor, especially Macquarie and Gibb, who was governor at the time of Bungaree's death.

Matthew Flinders regarded Bungaree as a 'brave and worthy fellow', and all diarists and journalists of that period mentioned him, mostly in reference to his manly character and effervescent personality. On board ship and as part of Sydney society, he became popular also for his ingenious characterisations of the governor and other leading figures of the day.

Bungaree adjusted much better than the unfortunate Bennelong to white society, possibly because his family group remained supportive. The government of the day gave him a brass breastplate on which were carved the words 'Bungaree, King of the Blacks'. This he proudly wore. His wife Gooseberry was also recognised as a worthy identity, and she too was given an inscribed breastplate to wear.

Many significant eulogies were spoken and written in the local papers when Bungaree died. Research has revealed that he was buried in the vicinity of what is now the Royal Sydney Golf Course. (It is surprising that a commemorative plaque has not been erected there.)

Wylie

In 1841 a young Aboriginal man from Albany in Western Australia, known as Wylie, was chosen to accompany Edward John Eyre as a guide on his historic exploratory journey across South Australia. A white man named Baxter and three other Aboriginal men later joined Eyre and Wylie on the second leg of this journey, which was to be from Fowlers Bay, South Australia, to Albany.

Travelling conditions soon became extremely difficult due to lack of water. To make matters worse, Baxter and the new Aboriginal members of the group proved to be in bitter and constant opposition. Finally, a brawl erupted between these men, all of whom were suffering from dehydration, hunger and thirst, and Baxter was killed. The three Aboriginal recruits realised that there would be repercussions and absconded, taking most of the food and ammunition with them. Wylie and Eyre were left unharmed, but the two then had an even more difficult task dogged by thirst and exhaustion as they continued determinedly along the planned route. In June, with Eyre near death, they came upon a French whaling ship anchored off the coast. The two rested on board for a fortnight and then, with additional supplies, continued on their way completing their journey on 7 July.

This expedition, although fraught with despair, proved successful in its geographical findings. On his return Eyre in his report noted that Wylie's 'behaviour in all circumstances was admirable', and stated that without Wylie's help he would never have been able to complete the journey.

Wylie, despite involvement such as this with the whites, remained totally loyal to his own people who respected him as a significant group member.

Jacky-Jacky

In the mid nineteenth century a young Aboriginal man named Jacky-Jacky was taken into white society in the Sydney area and taught to speak English. In 1848 E.B. Kennedy, who had befriended him, chose Jacky-Jacky to accompany his ill-fated expedition from Rockingham Bay to Cape York.

During the course of the trip the group was attacked by hostile Aborigines (the reasons are not known), and ten of the explorers were killed. Jacky-Jacky, another Aboriginal man, who later disappeared into the bush, and Kennedy, who was severely wounded, were spared.

Jacky-Jacky, who was Kennedy's friend as well as his guide, spent days trying to carry the ailing man to safety. When Kennedy finally died, Jacky-Jacky buried him and continued on alone to report to the ship that awaited the group at Albany. Here, obviously distressed, he told the authorities all that had happened. He was also able to give the geographic information that the expedition had sought to discover. He was awarded a silver breastplate for his loyalty and heroism.

His courage and sincerity, evident at other times as well, was later commemorated by a plaque which still remains in St. James Church, Sydney.

Yuranigh

Yuranigh, who came from the Lachlan Valley clan of the Wiradjuri group, was yet another noted explorers' guide of this era. After learning to speak English, he was asked to accompany Sir Thomas Mitchell and his party on their fourth inland exploratory trek in 1845.

Sir Thomas Mitchell had become surveyor–general on the death of John Oxley in 1828 and filled the position very capably. In addition to the several inland expeditions which he personally led, he was responsible for laying out many towns and organising much road-making and bridge building during his time of office.

The expedition party that Yuranigh joined was away for several months through 1845–46. It was a successful trek along the waterways of central New South Wales and Victoria, and the men returned to Sydney having gained much helpful geographic information.

In Mitchell's report of this, his final expedition, he described his guide Yuranigh as 'a man possessed of determined courage, resolution, intelligence and good judgement'. On his return, Yuranigh assisted the authorities in his

own area, the Central West, as an interpreter and adviser, but spent most of his time with his own people, to whom he became a trusted elder. In 1852 he died at Molong, New South Wales, where his grave is marked by four dendroglyphs. There is also a government-provided plaque which is inscribed: 'Yuranigh, a native of courage, honesty and fidelity'.

Almost all of the noted white explorers of this era included one or more Aboriginal scouts in their expedition parties. The ability to discover water and the general bush lore of the Aboriginal men was of great help to the less gifted white men.

The breastplate custom

One very significant feature of the early transitional era was the custom of issuing brass breastplates to Aborigines who had, for whatever reason, earned recognition from the white community of New South Wales. The custom was begun by Governor Lachlan Macquarie in 1816.

The plates were issued at a dinner held each year at Parramatta. A hundred and seventy-nine people attended the first feast and the number increased each year. Ten years later more than three hundred attended. Some Aboriginal identities were brought from as far away as Newcastle, Bathurst and the South Coast.

Through giving these dinners, the government of the day hoped to foster a better understanding between the two races in the Sydney region and other areas more distant. In addition, giving the plates was thought to be an appropriate way of rewarding loyalty or assistance given to the white people — whether to the police, to government officials or to settlers.

The plates were given to both men and women. Each bore the receiver's name, plus a title of 'King', 'Queen', 'Prince' or 'Chief'. The recipients appeared to be very proud of their new ornaments and wore them at the end of a string or chain around their neck. The officials who maintained this practice did it in the hope of bettering relationships, and certain benefits were obvious.

However, the system overall was not beneficial for many reasons. In Aboriginal culture there was no provision for any such uplifted position. Some elders did become revered and honoured because of their wisdom, compassion and so on, but they were never set apart in such a way. The phoney titles such as 'King', therefore, caused much discord. In most instances the services for which the plates had been awarded had not benefited the other group members, and many of the new 'heroes' were not appreciated at all by their own people. In addition, the practice presented the Aborigines as oddities and not persons of true substance. It was a very superficial way to repay a debt.

Some of those who received breastplates set up their own camp in the area of Sydney now known as the Domain. Jacky-Jacky, whose name had become a legend, and Bungaree and his wife Gooseberry were among them. During the 1820s the men from this group often gave boomerang-throwing exhibitions in Hyde Park.

Most of the breastplates issued were roughly the shape of a kidney and ranged in size from twelve by six centimetres to eighteen by twelve centimetres. The brass was usually about two millimetres thick.

The practice of issuing breastplates was discontinued in 1830 by Governor Darling, but unofficial feasts and awards were given for several more years at the Field of Mars in Sydney.

There is no official record of the names of all who received breastplates, but many country newspaper offices and historical societies have lists of those that were distributed in their particular areas. The relatively few plates that are still in existence are now held as relics in museums.

Fig. 8.2 Examples of breastplates awarded during the 19th century.

THE NINETEENTH CENTURY — A SYNOPSIS

Despite some peaceful contact between the two races as described previously, the nineteenth century was a time of continual unbridled violence against the Aboriginal people. A study of the police records and the newspapers of this era reveal that fierce and constant aggression towards them was rampant in all areas. There appears to have been very little attempt on the part of white colonists to understand the needs or customs of the indigenous people and even less attempt to treat them with even a pretence of justice.

Fig. 9.1 Aboriginal traditions and customs were seldom respected or understood by the white colonists in the nineteenth century.

© Australian Museum. Photo: W. Roth. 2162.

Reasons for conflict

Most Aboriginal attacks on the white population were retaliatory and almost always followed an incidence of deliberate persecution. The persecution took many forms. To begin with, the white men, using their guns, quickly commandeered the most arable land in the areas to which they came. In all instances the land they settled had, of course, been the major hunting ground of a local Aboriginal group. It had produced grass seeds for their dampers, wild fruits and other plant food as well as water. To make matters worse the colonists began to slaughter kangaroos and other animals in their hundreds so that the grazing land would be available for the new sheep and cattle. The Aboriginal people of all areas soon found it almost impossible to obtain enough food. It also became a common practice among the new white people to pretend friendship and then give the starving Aborigines flour and meat laced with strychnine, knowing that the whole group would share the proffered food. As a result fear and mistrust of the whites became evident everywhere.

Furthermore, many Aboriginal groups were forbidden on pain of death the use of the major freshwater areas, which were kept for the sheep and cattle. Unbelievably, then, in many areas the water that was left for them was deliberately poisoned. In some areas whole groups, thousands of people, were poisoned or left to die of thirst.

The colonists of each area quickly and wilfully desecrated the local sacred sites, such as bora grounds and burial areas. In most instances they refused to allow on pain of death any further Aboriginal access to these areas. This caused extreme trauma and despair for a people whose culture and kinship laws required ritual adherence to performing their spiritual ceremonies.

In addition any man or woman who was sighted on any section of the newly acquired 'white' land, for whatever reason, could expect to be shot. Others were relentlessly hunted down. 'Abo hunting', as it was then known, became a local sport in most areas. Many thousands of individuals faced frightening, lonely deaths in this way. Thousands more were wounded during this period and left to suffer without medical help.

In some areas, particularly in northern New South Wales and Queensland, the colonists chose terrorist tactics that were even more macabre and brutal. The Colonial Office of the time received many reports from white historians and humanitarians of the day attesting to the fact that Aboriginal men, women and children were being burned alive; others had their throats or genitals cut and then, for the entertainment of the whites were left to run and flap about till they collapsed. The Colonial Office registered but then ignored the stream of complaints.

In almost all areas the murder of individual Aborigines and even large-scale massacres were constant and quite premeditated. Such action was regarded by a large proportion of the white population as 'necessary' because the Aboriginal people were, after all, standing in the way of progress! Very seldom was the murder of an Aboriginal man or woman treated as a crime; nor was it, it seems, thought of with any sign of conscience or regret.

Some of the settlers carried the repression of the black race to an even more sickening degree. These people chose not to murder but attempted, through cruelty, to keep all Aborigines 'fearful of whites'. They taught this lesson very effectively by capturing individuals and small groups who were then systematically beaten and tortured. In hundreds of such instances Aboriginal men and women had their limbs broken and/or their hands, ears or fingers severed. After the torture these people would be set 'free' to bear witness to the 'superiority' of the new white race. Records of many such atrocities can be found in the historical journal, *Records of Times Past* and in the Colonial Office records as well as in the hearts and minds of the victims' descendants.

In addition to the constant violence and persecution there was an over-riding fear within all Aboriginal groups for the safety of their women, many thousands of whom were forcibly abducted and sexually abused. Hundreds of Aboriginal girls and women were beaten or murdered during or after being violated. Hundreds of others were left to cope in the best way they could, with the subsequent birth of a child.

In the following pages there are brief details from documented records of just a few of the many thousands of murders and massacres that occurred across Australia during the nineteenth century. The accounts presented epitomise the overall viciousness and depravity of many of the new colonists. It is difficult to find words to describe adequately the despair, the confusion and the desperation of the Aboriginal people during this period of their history.

The Pinjarra incident

During the 1820s, as white settlers first ventured into the Swan River area of Western Australia, there was constant and bitter conflict. In one instance in 1829 a man called Budge was killed and fairly soon afterwards, another named Morell was badly injured by Aboriginal men. (The circumstances that precipitated these attacks were not recorded.) Following these two incidents, a large group of armed white men, including police, soldiers and several local citizens, went forth to do battle with the Aboriginal group which was then camped near the site of the town of Pinjarra. This particular group had around eighty members, including the women and children, most of whom would have known nothing about the attacks. The white 'army' made a surprise raid. Their attack was brutal and vicious. When it concluded, the Police Captain lay dead, as did most of the Aboriginal people.

The few Aboriginal survivors, mainly women and children, most of whom were wounded, were dragged away and imprisoned. They were not permitted to bury their dead, which would have been extremely stressful to them. The records do not show how these people fared in prison. It is known that none of them returned to their original campsite.

The Yagan incident

An incident occurred in Western Australia in 1831 that was also long remembered. It involved a young Aboriginal man named Yagan, who belonged to a group which lived then in the area where Perth stands today.

Yagan first came to the notice of the white community when he was sentenced to be hanged for the retaliatory murder of a man named Gase. Yagan had a striking appearance with a proud and noble bearing. He was rescued from the gallows by a young official named Robert Lyon. In a government-funded experiment, Lyon was to teach Yagan English and then work with him towards securing peace between the two races.

Within time Lyon achieved this goal with Yagan, who was an obvious leader, proving to be most cooperative. Eventually Yagan was released from the island where he had been taken and permitted to return to his people.

Before leaving the island, Yagan and Robert Lyon, who had developed a deep friendship, had agreed to work for a truce between the two races. For several months there was peace in the area, and it was hoped that with further cooperation from both sides, peace would continue. It was not to be.

Within a year there was more friction. It came about after an incident where a band of renegade whites had come upon a gathering of Aboriginal men, women and children and without provocation had fired on them at random. Several of the defenceless group were killed immediately. Most others were wounded. No medical help was offered or given, and the men responsible were never brought to trial.

These people were Yagan's kin and, as this massacre was a repeat of the brutal repression they had all previously experienced, Yagan considered that the truce he had honoured had been broken. He subsequently led his men to yet another retaliatory raid, during which his own father and several other men were captured and executed. Yagan managed to elude capture on this occasion, but several months later he was betrayed by two white men to whom he had earlier given assistance.

Before this incident Yagan had become respected and well liked by many of the local whites, and there was a strong protest by many, including his friend Robert Lyon, when he was recaptured and subsequently hanged without a trial. Some new settlers were finally beginning to perceive the racial injustice of this era and the sickening effect of perpetual retaliation.

Many people, both black and white, were further disturbed when white officials had Yagan's head cut off and mummified before being exhibited as a curiosity in all the capital cities of Australia and in London. In addition, strips of Yagan's skin were taken from his body and sold at auction as souvenirs. Historical records reveal that practices such as these were then not uncommon. Some such 'trophies' are still in various collections.

The Myall Creek massacre

In 1831 there was racial unrest throughout most areas of New South Wales. One well-documented incident occurred at Myall Creek, near the town of Inverell.

Following the death of two white men, both speared on separate occasions, many white settlers became angry and panic-stricken. The local authorities were attempting to investigate both the murders and the reasons behind them when several settlers and other anti-black identities decided to take matters into their own hands. These men armed themselves with guns and other weapons and rode out to Myall Creek, which was the nearest Aboriginal campsite. There with guns drawn they captured twenty-eight people, including women and children.

The members of this particular Aboriginal group were on friendly terms with the white people who lived in their immediate vicinity and could speak pidgin English well enough to be understood. They protested their innocence. They explained that they personally knew nothing of the previous killings. (This could well have been true for there were several Aboriginal groups in that area.) Some white settlers who witnessed their capture protested on their behalf as well, but despite this, the twenty-eight were tied together and forcibly taken to a remote spot further along the Myall Creek bank. There, while still tied together, each of the twenty-eight, including the children, was viciously and systematically beaten to death. The twenty-eight mutilated bodes were left where they fell.

The white band responsible for this massacre was also responsible for two earlier instances of mass murder of Aborigines.

The Myall Creek massacre was yet another example of the horrifying brutality towards Aborigines that prevailed. However, it remains unique in this era not because of its brutality but because the local authorities did not on this occasion condone the behaviour. Seven of the white men responsible were subsequently brought to trial, found guilty of murder and hanged.

Although many white citizens, including most sections of the clergy and Governor Gipps himself, could see the justice in this verdict, there was much opposition to it from major newspapers, namely the *Herald* and the *Australian*. The papers had taken this stand because hundreds of other white men in other areas were not being brought to trial for similar crimes. And even though 'justice was seen to be done' in this instance, it did not alleviate the problems of the few members of the group who had avoided capture. The lives of the few survivors without their hunters, elders and protectors would have been indescribably sad, fearful and difficult.

The Benalla incident

In 1837 near the town of Benalla in Victoria two brothers, George and William Faithful, were moving their sheep to new farmlands further south when several Aboriginal men attacked and killed both of them and their shepherds. (The circumstances that had prompted this attack were not recorded.) This was one of the first signs of Aboriginal uprising or retaliation in this area, and the white settlers, with official permission, reacted in a fierce and extreme manner.

A chosen band of armed men determinedly tracked down as many of the local Aboriginal people as possible. They made no attempt to discover which of these people, if any, had been responsible for the previous killings or why. They simply and systematically shot each one they captured on the spot.

The exact number of Aboriginal deaths was never officially recorded, but it was estimated to be between twenty and thirty. As with the Myall Creek massacre, the remnants of this Aboriginal group, the few who had managed to elude capture, would have been left in a tragic state suffering extreme grief, fear, isolation and starvation.

Incidents such as this were repeated over and over again across most of Australia.

Windradyne of the Wiradjuri

A young Aboriginal man called Windradyne became well known to the white community in the early nineteenth century. He belonged to a clan of the Wiradjuri who occupied the land where Bathurst in New South Wales now stands.

European settlers first came to this lush pastoral area in 1812. By 1820

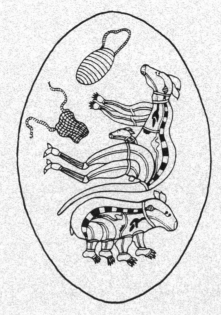

their numbers had increased dramatically, and they had taken possession of almost all the arable land as well as the watering places. They showed little regard for the local Aboriginal people whose lives they had disrupted. Aggression towards the Aborigines increased month by month. Many settlers gave them food laced with poison or blatantly shot to kill whenever one or a group of them was sighted.

Windradyne, their young leader, was captured in 1822 while attempting to rescue a small group of his people who had been unlawfully taken into custody. He was a tall, extremely strong man, and it took six soldiers plus a blow from a musket, which broke several of his ribs, before he was subdued.

Once captured the authorities decided to make an example of him, and he was kept in chains for a month, despite protests from a few fair-minded members of the white community. During his imprisonment, other groups of settlers from that area continued to blatantly murder, torture and terrorise his people. The white man's law offered no protection.

Consequently, when Windradyne was finally released, he quickly organised and then led a group of his men in a retaliatory raid. They planned to face up to a group of whites who were meeting that night at a place known in the area as the 'Murdering Hut'. It was so named because many of Windradyne's people had been taken there on previous occasions, subjected to all sorts of indecencies and then murdered. Windradyne's raid was successful. Seven white men — the seven he had gone after — were killed. Significantly, only those men who had been directly responsible for previous Aboriginal deaths were killed. Other white men were accosted but spared on that same night.

Following this daring incident, official reprisals were swift in coming and extremely vicious. Martial law was declared, and the local soldiers, police and settlers were given a totally free rein; that is, they were given official permission to murder or maim every Aborigine they could find with no questions asked.

Most of the local men quickly began their brutal campaign, and a reward was offered for the recapture of Windradyne. After witnessing the relentless destruction of his people for several months, Windradyne, hoping to bring it to an end, finally came in to negotiate.

His subsequent trial aroused much interest as some of the settlers in the area had come to realise that he was a proud and noble leader who had organised such retaliatory action in a vain effort to defend his people. His trial was long and complicated. Some members of the white community argued forcefully that he should be hanged; others argued against it. Eventually he was pardoned.

For Windradyne, however, there was no joy in this decision. By the time he was released most of his people had been either murdered or driven from the area. He died shortly afterwards, dispirited and alone.

The site of his grave is maintained to this day by the descendants of William Suttor, one of the white settlers whom he had met but spared on the night of the 'Murdering Hut' raid. (This information comes from a book entitled *Windradyne of the Wiradjuri* by P.J. Glessos.)

The Queensland massacres

There were spasmodic outbursts of racial conflict in Queensland from the time of the first European settlement, but the tragic massacres of both whites and blacks in the following account added greatly to the fast-growing fear and distress in that area.

In 1861 nineteen white people, comprising several whole families, were killed in a surprise Aboriginal raid. The news shocked everyone. The murder victims were settler families who had come only two weeks earlier to the area now known as the Darling Downs. The premeditated attack surprised the authorities as these particular people had appeared to make sincere attempts to befriend the local Aboriginal people. The attack was more organised than ever before. In addition, it was one of the very few occasions when white children were slain by Aboriginal aggressors.

The people from the local Aboriginal groups, most of whom could speak a little English, declared that they knew nothing of the attack. They too were disturbed by the ferocity of it. They and the authorities thought that the massacre was the work of a young renegade group of Aborigines who had recently begun such guerrilla-type activities. These young men had earlier been associated with the local police but after becoming disillusioned with police activities they had defiantly deserted and turned renegade. They firmly believed that violence was the only answer to the rampant injustice of the day. This aggressive attitude was alien to the original Aboriginal philosophy, and their actions were not generally supported by their own people.

The history of other oppressed races reveals that the emergence of a guerrilla group such as this is an expected by-product. If it were not for the extreme control and wisdom of most of the Aboriginal elders of this period, there would have been a great many more similar groups.

The authorities were unable to locate the members of the renegade group for questioning, and the disquiet and fear of the white community mounted daily. Eventually a group of militant settlers decided to take control of the situation and to solve it in their own way. They planned their course of action and armed themselves accordingly. They then began a program of total annihilation of the Aboriginal people.

They began determinedly and cold-bloodedly to murder or drive away every Aboriginal man, woman and child in the whole central Queensland area. They kept up their systematic onslaught until they felt they had achieved their goal.

It is not known exactly how many Aboriginal people died during this ruthless massacre or whether the renegades were killed too, but overall several entire groups were totally wiped out within a few weeks. This involved the murder of several hundred innocent people. The fate of the relatively few survivors, all displaced, fearful and totally traumatised, is not known.

The Eugowra incident

In 1896, at Eugowra, New South Wales, there was a massacre of a different kind. The Aboriginal people of this area, a clan of the Wiradjuri, were then experiencing a complete cultural breakdown of the kind that inevitably followed white settlement.

This area had been relatively free of the shame of mass murder and brutality towards the Aboriginal people, but other factors combined just as convincingly to create an alarming situation. The white pioneers were arriving in great numbers determined to farm the land. To this effect they had taken over all the waterways and the plains that had previously been the hunting grounds of the local Aborigines.

The Aboriginal people had consequently become desperately short of food and water and, in addition, had been forced to abandon many of their previous ritual practices. The situation was very stressful. Furthermore, many Aboriginal women had become closely involved with some of the white trappers, farmers and shepherds. Some had formed lasting relationships, ignoring their age-old marriage and moiety ties.

The elders had no answers for their restless, disturbed people and they were fast losing control of their clan. Furthermore, white men's diseases and the introduction of alcohol were having a devastating effect. The combined result was conflict within the group, which in turn added to the ever-growing resentment, misunderstandings and feeling of hopelessness which had begun to overshadow the life of the group.

One day the evident despair and distress finally came to a head, and the members of the group began fighting among themselves. The fighting became fierce, vicious and tragic. As darkness fell almost every man, woman and child was either dead or dying. Some lay injured on the ground, and others had climbed into the branches of high trees to die. Concerned settlers offered assistance to the few survivors, all of whom were ultimately taken to the Condobolin mission.

A disturbing occurrence such as this was alien in every way to the customs and principles of the original Wiradjuri culture. It was certainly precipitated by the overwhelming pressure created by the loss of their sacred land, their livelihood and their traditional totem ties.

Throughout Australia during this turbulent time there were many other tragic instances of self-destruction. It is still happening today!

The white invasion of Tasmania

The first white settlement in Tasmania began in 1803 at Risdon Cove on the Derwent River. It began as a convict settlement, but many free English settlers quickly followed. They immediately began to build homes and to claim and cultivate the best of the land.

Tension between the settlers and the Aborigines developed for the worst, right from the start. For thousands of years, Aboriginal people of Tasmania had been secure in the knowledge that they, like the trees and all other living creatures, were part of a never-ending growth pattern. They believed that the land where they lived belonged to each of them and, equally, and even more significantly, they belonged to it. How could such a people understand the white man's need for individual possession and domination?

The white population in Tasmania continued to grow in number and spread quickly. Within just a few years most of the best land was taken over, and hundreds of Aboriginal people had been ruthlessly murdered. Those who had survived had been driven from the plains into the mountain wilderness where conditions were freezing in winter. The remnant of the Aboriginal population protested with occasional outbursts of violence. Unfortunately this merely made matters worse because it increased the bitterness against them, and their primitive spears were in no way a match for the muskets and strychnine of the white men.

Not the least of the shameful deeds on record was the Black Line organised by Governor Arthur in 1830. It was his written intention to seek out and murder absolutely every Aboriginal man, woman and child in the south-eastern part of the island. In the effort to do so he led two thousand settlers and soldiers, each walking one metre apart. But the indigenous black people won this battle. The exercise cost £35 000, and the two thousand chosen men traipsed through bush for seven weeks but found only one frightened old woman and a small boy. Sadly though, this seeming triumph did little to ease the overall situation, which continued to worsen.

During this turbulent period, several white groups, led by George Augustus Robertson, were attempting to rally support for the Aborigines. In 1831 their voice was finally heard and Robertson was given official permission and finance to create a colony for the few surviving people on Flinders Island in Bass Strait.

On the surface the project appeared to have merit, and many concerned white people in the area applauded the idea. Unfortunately neither George Robertson nor his supporters could understand that each Aboriginal person had an unshakeable affinity with their own geographic area. This was an almost supernatural tie, a tie that had controlled their lives and those of their ancestors for centuries. For these people to resettle was not a simple matter. Yet within four years almost every surviving member of the Tasmanian Aboriginal population had been located and persuaded, most against their will, to go to Flinders Island.

At the Flinders Island colony well-meaning efforts were made to resettle them, to make them 'civilised' in the white way. However, the scheme failed dismally. The Aboriginal people were simply not able to adjust to this change in their way of life. They were filled with despair, frustration and depression; they had lost their land, their pride, their heritage, their very reason for living. In addition, they appeared to have very little resistance to the diseases of the white race.

Despite all efforts to the contrary, one by one the Aboriginal people began to die. By 1847 only forty-four of the original number were still alive. This confused little group was eventually resettled in better premises at Oyster Bay, near Hobart. The situation there did not improve, and the people continued to die. By 1869 there were only two of them left alive, William Lanne and Truganini.

William Lanne, the last direct-descent Tasmanian Aboriginal male, died the following year. Truganini lived on until 1876.

Truganini

Truganini is the best known of all the Tasmanian Aborigines who lived in the traditional period. She was born the year that white settlement began in Tasmania — 1803.

By the time she was seventeen years old, she had witnessed the murder of hundreds of her people, including her mother, her uncle and her husband-to-be. In addition, she had seen her sisters and her stepmother beaten and kidnapped and been violated herself. She had seen the hunting grounds of all of their sacred areas ruthlessly taken.

Records reveal that she was a diminutive girl, a mere 145 centimetres tall, who was extremely attractive and spirited when she was young. She had learned to speak English early in her life, and her intelligence and wit often astounded those who met her.

As a young woman, she assisted George Robertson as he persuaded her people to leave their area and form a colony on Flinders Island. Death and disaster awaited them if they refused! She reasoned that assimilation was preferable to destruction, and so she worked hard to help her people find a new life.

The subsequent failure of the Flinders Island experiment and then the Oyster Bay settlement were personal tragedies for her. During the later years of her life she was treated kindly, but her final years as the only Aboriginal survivor were lonely and bewildering.

She died in 1876 pleading that her body not be used for experimental purposes, as were those of others of her race. Despite the promises given, however, her body was scientifically analysed, and her bones actually lay on exhibition in the Hobart Museum for exactly a hundred years. In 1976 after much consultation her remains were cremated as was the custom of her ancestors. Her ashes were then scattered on the sea. Belatedly, those present at this ceremony paid homage to this courageous and much-wronged lady. The tragic life of Truganini echoes that of her people.

It was thought at first that Truganini was the very last of the direct-descent Aborigines of Tasmania, but another woman was later discovered living on Kangaroo Island. She had been abducted and taken there by sealers while very young. When this woman died in 1888 it was the end of the direct-descent race.

The Aboriginal people had lived on the island now known as Tasmania generation after generation, for more than ten thousand years. Less than eighty-five years after white habitation, however, their long-standing tie with the natural and spiritual forces of their land had almost ceased to exist.

There are, of course, several thousand mixed-descent people who live today in Tasmania, mainly on the offshore islands. Many are now working to preserve their Aboriginal heritage and trying to discover more than is generally known of the culture and history of their ancestors.

Sealers

During the nineteenth century hundreds of sealers, men who trapped and killed seals in order to sell their pelts, lived bleak, semi-outcast lives in the

144

cold regions off the Tasmanian coast. Men of many nationalities, including Europeans, Asians and islanders, made their living in this way. Records reveal that generally they were extremely brutal to the Tasmanian Aborigines, particularly the women. Many women, most of whom were expert at diving, swimming, fishing and catching seals, were abducted by sealers and forced to live as slaves with the sealers using their diving skills. They were also sexually abused and many were beaten and murdered. This is yet another tragic aspect in the history of these people.

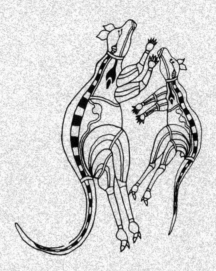

Traditional living disbanded

Records show that throughout Australia 270 white people, mostly men, died as a direct result of the black/white conflict. This is indeed a disturbing statistic, yet if one delves deeper into Australia's black history one discovers that more than two hundred and fifty thousand Aboriginal people — more than half the original population — were murdered.

There was peace of a kind by the end of the nineteenth century. On the surface law and order appeared to prevail; the uncontrolled killing had almost ceased. Australia, as one of a group of British colonies, was developing at a very rapid rate. The convict system had been abolished in 1868, and hitherto unknown areas of the country had been explored. The colonists had taken over the arable areas and constructed roads to link all the major settlements and many of the outlying areas.

Thousands of large towns were flourishing in coastal and rural areas, and there were hundreds of smaller outback settlements. Coal-mining was well established, and many factory and home industries were developing rapidly. Farming regions all over the country were progressing well and becoming extremely productive. Coach and rail routes were being extended to cater for the rapidly expanding population. Gold had been discovered in 1851, bringing thousands of people of all nationalities to New South Wales and Victoria.

Schools and hospitals were available in all larger towns and were becoming increasingly accessible in many rural areas. Education, however, was provided for white children only; Aboriginal children, including those of 'mixed' parentage, were generally not permitted to attend state schools. This factor added much to the frustration and bitterness of the Aboriginal people and greatly hindered their adjustment to mission living and integration into white society.

Newspaper offices had been established everywhere, and the several colonies and territories of Australia were about to become a federation.

Much 'white' progress was indeed obvious. But what of the Aboriginal people? As the twentieth century dawned, the cause of these people — which was merely to maintain their previous lifestyle — had become hopeless. And most Aboriginal people had reluctantly come to realise the fact. Many traditional groups had already been destroyed, and the way of life and culture of those who remained had irretrievably broken down.

By 1910 the structure of most of the Aboriginal groups as disciplined, self-maintained units had completely ceased to be, with the exception of a minority situated in remote areas of northern, Western and Central Australia. In a little more than a hundred years, more than forty thousand years of dedicated, ordered living, of the spiritual and cultural build-up of a thriving, vibrant people, had been swept aside almost as if it had never existed. The Aboriginal population had been reduced to far less than half its size, and the surviving people found themselves displaced, unwanted and struggling desperately to adjust to a new and alien way of life.

In addition they had been forced to subjugate their pride and their spirit — but they had not lost them; not quite. Despite unrelenting persecution and near genocide, their pride and their spirit as a people who would survive continued to burn within.

The nineteenth century had been tragic and traumatic for the Aboriginal people in all areas of Australia. In the beginning of the twentieth century there was peace and progress of a kind, but the price for the Aboriginal people had been inestimably high.

The period broadly spanning those years from the first European settlement until the 1960s has been called the transitional period of Aboriginal history. It was for them a time of continual change, trauma and distress. As the nineteenth century came to a close most Aboriginal people — no longer able to successfully continue their traditional lifestyle — had been forced to accept one of two alternatives: mission life or integration. Only a very few groups in isolated areas of Central and northern Australia were able to continue a semi-traditional lifestyle.

 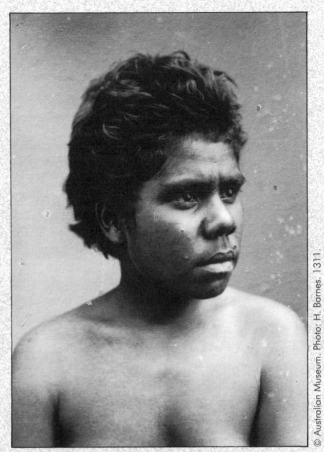

© Australian Museum. Photo: H. Barnes. 1311.

Fig. 9.2 With the arrival of white colonists came the beginning of a century-long disruption of life and tradition for the Aboriginal people. Today they still struggle to regain their identity.

Mission life

During the second half of the nineteenth century and into the twentieth century, most Aboriginal families — in many instances, all remaining members of a previously self-contained group — were forcibly taken to a government-provided reserve. Many were taken there in chains.

The reserves became known as missions in most areas due to the association and support of the Christian churches. Throughout the transitional period, more than three hundred and fifty such reserves were set up in areas all around Australia. The mission founders intended that basic shelter, food and clothing, as well as medical and emotional support, would be provided. All this read well on paper but, in reality, the missions failed dismally in most areas. The reasons were many.

Each one was set up and run on the lines of a prison camp. Little provision was made for basic human needs, and no consideration was given to the rights of individuals.

Many of the people were taken to a mission far distant from their home area. This was very disturbing because of their deep and sacred bonding with their own land. To die outside one's area was tantamount to losing one's soul.

Several separate groups were often housed together. In many instances the people of these groups would speak a different language and their religious and cultural backgrounds would differ markedly, which of course added to the tension and confusion. The food in all missions was very basic, different from what the people were used to and almost always in short supply. Alcohol was given as a reward.

The accommodation was alien. Missions were grossly overcrowded, with little or no provision for privacy or recreation. There was constant mismanagement in most missions with blatant and sometimes extreme dishonesty on the part of white officials. Some were also extremely brutal giving harsh beatings for minor misdemeanors. Many Aboriginal people suffered severe and irreversible depression, which manifested itself in a disturbing state of mental and physical malaise. Money and provisions were always short, due in many instances to the dishonest management.

The forced change of lifestyle produced serious medical problems, particularly viral chest complaints and ear and eye infections. In addition, the people had little immunity to white diseases with which they now came into contact, and common, minor ailments such as measles proved fatal in many instances.

All aspects of their traditional culture and religion, especially the ritual and sacred ceremonies, were viewed by white officials as heathen and degrading. Any adherence to such practices was fervently discouraged and punished. Even the speaking of one's former language was a punishable offence.

No mission Aborigine had any legal rights whatsoever. They had no say in what happened to them or to their children. They were legally powerless. This is a dehumanising situation for any people, even more so for those who had previously enjoyed close extended family and communal support. During this period thousands of Aboriginal children were forcibly taken from their mission parents, whose pleadings and protests were totally ignored. These children were then brought up in government run institutions. Most of them were never reunited with their parents. This situation caused great consternation, sadness and lasting bitterness.

It is a national tragedy that the Aboriginal missions were not more honestly and more sensibly organised. Had this been so, decades of extreme misery and misunderstanding might have been alleviated — a little. Most Aboriginal people who can still remember the old reserve days speak of the experience with fear and dismay. The standard of life that Aboriginal people were forced to endure in the early missions will forever be a cause of shame in Australia's history.

One of the most distressing factors is that the tens of thousands of Aboriginal children who grew up on these reserves were given little — in most cases no — formal English education. This situation continued until the 1950s.

Although there are some exceptions where the standard of living is still degrading, the decades since the 1960s have brought vast improvements in most reserve areas. The Aboriginal people in most areas today have their own elected representatives who organise and control. State governments provide housing, that is, an adequate home for each family, with water and sewerage connections. Health services and recreational facilities are also government-funded, although many are still being inadequately administered.

Schooling to tertiary level has finally become readily available to all Aboriginal children, and this is a major advance. The members of most Aboriginal communities are now forming their own co-operatives and doing what they each can by providing labour, suggestions and so on to assist the drive for progress. A renaissance has finally begun, but there is still a long, long way to go!

Integration

Some Aboriginal people chose, during the trauma of the early twentieth century, to find employment in white society rather than accept the imprisonment and subsequent degradation of mission living. A lack of formal education in English, plus a natural feeling of insecurity, hindered the first of them in this quest. And if they did obtain employment they were not paid the same wages as their white co-workers. This, of course, helped to further lower their standard of living.

Despite the obvious difficulties, many of them persevered. These Aboriginal pioneers must be given great credit for their courage and vision. They certainly faced a fearfully difficult task.

In the early stages, because of a lack of other training, most Aboriginal men were able only to take farm-hand or stockmen jobs on farming properties, or labouring jobs in the larger towns and cities. The Aboriginal women were employed mainly to do domestic duties. Again this was the only training they had been given.

As the second and third generation of twentieth-century Aboriginal people followed, however, those seeking work and integration have ventured on to many more varied and interesting careers — particularly those relatively few who had been fortunate enough to receive a formal English education.

During the transitional period, the obvious problems of integration were compounded further by constant racial and social friction due to differing cultures, religion and family allegiances. This friction was intensified by the many mixed marriages that inevitably followed the mingling of the two peoples. (Thomas Keneally's *The Chant of Jimmy Blacksmith*, also filmed, epitomises the social traumas and misunderstandings of this time.)

Further tensions and frustrations were caused because the majority of Aboriginal children, including those of mixed parentage, were barred from attending their local state school. This was the legal situation all over Australia until the 1950s. This is hard to comprehend when one considers that up to and including the 1940s, thousands of Aboriginal men had answered the call to defend their country in World Wars I and II. They were considered equal to this task, it seems, yet the children they left behind were being forbidden, simply because they were Aboriginal, to attend their local school.

Furthermore, it was not until 1962 that laws were finally passed which ensured that Aborigines, whatever their occupation, would be paid the same wage as other workers. And it was even later, after the 1967 referendum, before Aboriginal people were counted in the Australian census and therefore recognised as Australian citizens with the right to vote.

It can be easily understood, therefore, why integration in the first half of the twentieth century was extremely difficult for any person of Aboriginal descent. In most instances it was almost impossible.

In the 1990s there are thousands of Aboriginal men and women working at all levels, in all professions, in all spheres of multicultural Australian society. Even so the high level of unemployment among Aboriginal people is still a problem that needs to be addressed. However the current provision of educational facilities for all Aboriginal children is a force which augurs well for the future.

A

contemporary

focus

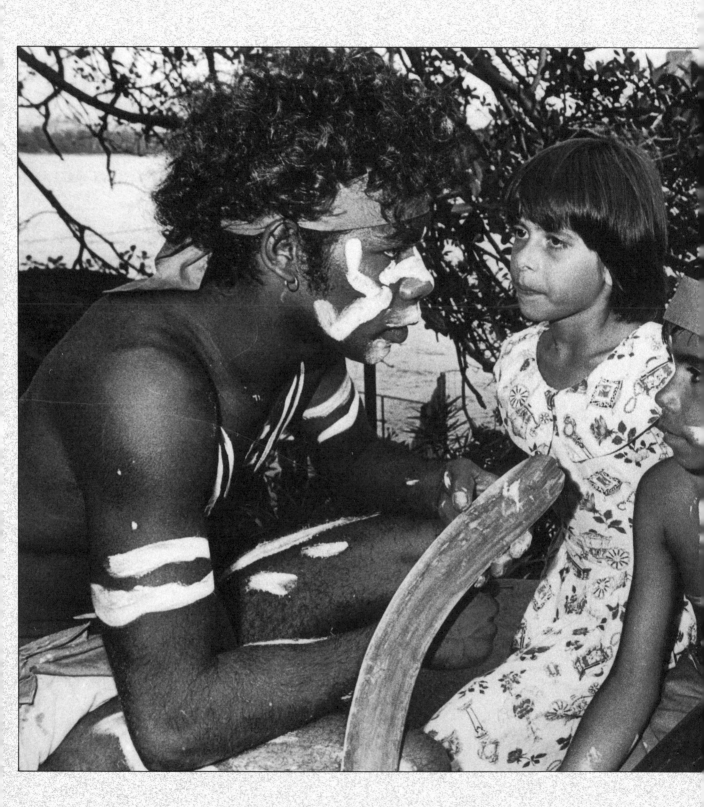

THE CONTEMPORARY SITUATION

The contemporary situation in the Aboriginal community is both disturbing and yet exciting. Many long-awaited changes, touching on all spheres of Aboriginal life, have been realised during the 1970s and 1980s. This is encouraging. The burgeoning renewal of Aboriginal identity and creativity has most certainly begun — but much has yet to be achieved. There needs to be a continual tidal wave of change throughout Australia.

Fig. 10.1 Children of mixed cultures can now face the future with hope.

John Fairfax Group P/L. Photo courtesy Mitchell Library, State Library of N.S.W.

153

A study of the contemporary Aboriginal community (1.04% of the Australian population) reveals a people united in spirit with a nationwide quest for recognition of their separate identities, abilities and rights. Although this union is strong and obvious, the people themselves live quite diversified lives. There are more than four thousand who continue to live a semi-traditional life in areas known as home stations in Queensland, the Northern Territory, Western Australia and Central Australia. There are those whose lives are similar to those of the white community as regards lifestyle, housing and so on, yet they reside in all-Aboriginal settlements. There are many thousands more who live as one with the rest of Australia's multicultural urban population.

The personalities, careers, educational standards, hopes and aspirations of individual people might differ, but the determined loyalty of Aboriginal people to the cause of their survival and acceptance is nationwide and inspiring.

Land rights in the 1990s

Most contemporary Aboriginal people feel that their ultimate survival and acceptance will come through the granting of land rights.

The land rights issue is not widely understood by non-Aborigines, and the push towards this goal has been frought with difficulties. From an Aboriginal perspective the term *land rights* simply means the (non-restrictive) return of viable land bases where the Aboriginal people of each area can work to regenerate their communities, economies and culture and be self-determining in their religions and social choices.

The Australian Government, with the support of the Australian people, needs to negotiate a process for achieving a suitable land settlement based on justice. Only then can a reconciliation, a healing of past injustices and differences, begin and grow. Some progress has been made.

In the late 1980s Federal Parliament recognised that the Aboriginal people had and have prior ownership and possession, and that the concept of 'terra nullius' (that the first colonists came to an empty land) did not apply. During the 1988 annual national gathering of Aboriginal leaders the then prime minister, Bob Hawke, publically acknowledged Aboriginal entitlement to freehold land. At this gathering he committed his government to negotiate a treaty, acknowledging that Australia is the only former British colony that has no formal treaty with its indigenous people.

When will such a treaty become a legal reality? How will the land that has been promised be distributed? How much land? Will it be granted in all regions or only some? These and many other questions are waiting to be answered.

Fig. 10.2 This drawing by Aboriginal artist Billy Reid shows skill in capturing the human emotion and the vibrant atmosphere of outback Australia.

C H A P T E R E L E V E N

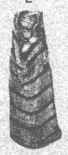

ABORIGINAL POETRY

During the 1980s many Aboriginal authors have seen their work published and widely read, and many Aboriginal playwrights have seen their work produced effectively on stage. We are approaching an enlightened era where white Australia is finally beginning to ponder and to probe more deeply the undeniable black heritage of their land.

Foremost among the fast-growing list of Aboriginal authors are the poets. Aboriginal poetry is reflective, emotional, honest and different. Each poem makes a forceful, social and emotional comment.

Fig. 11.1 A portrait of Kevin Gilbert taken by Eleanor Williams.

The thirty poems presented here bring to the surface many contemporary issues; the exciting as well as the disturbing aspects. There are also those that echo the past, both the traditional and the transitional. Fifteen poems have come from the noted Aboriginal poet and author, the late Kevin Gilbert. Thirteen other Aboriginal poets have also contributed. They are:

Julie Watson Nungarrayi	Mary Duroux
Stephen Clayton	Robert Walker
W. Les Russell	Eva Johnson
Oodgeroo Noonuccal (Kath Walker)	Gerry Bostock
Jack Davis	Frank Doolan
Hyllus Maris	Daisy Utemorrah
Maureen Watson	

The poems presented here were selected from the book *Inside Black Australia: An Anthology of Aboriginal Poetry*. It was published in 1988 by Penguin Books Australia and was reprinted in 1989. It contains 143 poems from forty-four Aboriginal authors. Kevin Gilbert contributed to and edited the book.

Kevin Gilbert

Kevin Gilbert was born black in Condobolin, New South Wales, on 10 July 1933. He was the youngest of eight children with direct Aboriginal, Irish and English descendancy. His Aboriginal people are the Wiradjuri of New South Wales. Kevin, together with a large number of other Wiradjuri descendants, communicated aspects of their culture and way of life. In addition, the group safely preserved many original artefacts and implements.

Kevin's early years were happy and secure. He was orphaned at the age of seven, having lost both parents in the space of a few months. His childhood from that point changed radically. He spent an unhappy period in an orphanage, then began a series of moves with his older sisters to and from various lean-to-shelters in different Aboriginal fringe settlements — the only alternative. His older brothers were away on active service in World War II. At the time (the 1940s) there were few job opportunities in any area for Aboriginal people, and those who did manage to find work received only a fraction of the wage paid to their white co-workers. There were no pensions, no social security payments and no special support for orphaned children. Furthermore, in most cases black children were refused admission to their local school (including those of mixed parentage). Any

158

adult who appeared to have an Aboriginal heritage was not counted in the census or allowed to vote — despite the fact that thousands of them were serving in the armed forces at the time.

Kevin was forced to leave school in grade 4 of primary school. His education before this had only been very sketchy, so there seemed little point in persevering. He needed money for food and so he worked as a cherry-picker, a rabbit-trapper and a collector of empty bottles, dead wool, scraps of metal and so on. He worked anywhere, at any time. He worked whenever at whatever he could. Throughout his teenage years he consciously fought against the shackles imposed on him by poverty and inequality — but life continued to be harsh and difficult.

Like many Aboriginal men and women of his generation, Keven Gilbert served many years in prison, which gave him access to library books. In this way he was able to improve his education greatly. During his imprisonment Kevin became fired with a fierce and embittered passion to fight for the rights of his fellow Aboriginal people in every area of life. This aim he pursued relentlessly, using his many talents.

Kevin Gilbert in the 1990s was a deep-thinking, hard-working family man who had the widespread respect and acknowledgement of both the black and the white communities. He was a very forceful political lobbyist, an author and poet of international acclaim, an artist, a tireless organiser and a much sought-after speaker at local, state and national Aboriginal conferences. In addition he was committed to advancing the cause of land rights and to furthering the work of the Aboriginal Community Aid organisation.

His published works include: *The Cherry Pickers, Because a White Man'll Never Do It, Living Black, People are Legends, The Blackside and Other Poems, Flashes of Essence: Poems in Person* (poetry readings on cassette), *Child's Dreaming, Black from the Edge* and *Aboriginal Sovereignty* (a document on land rights). In addition, he contributed to and edited *Inside Black Australia: An Anthology of Contemporary Aboriginal Poetry.*

The fifteen poems by Kevin Gilbert presented on the following pages have been selected for this book from *Inside Black Australia, People Are Legends* and *The Blackside and Other Poems.*

Old Man Biamanga

Old man
Biamanga
you took them into
the heart of the mountain
showed them wondrous things
not seen before
by men who were not men
until they were made men
by initiation and
truth of the Law
into the mountain you took them
and gave them the truth
and the spirit of life
and the Tree

Now you are gone
loggers climb Mumbulla Mountain
with the powersaws roaring in barbaric glee
there's shouts and there's laughter
'It's jake Jack it's apples
it's sweet mate it's bonza
and timber oh timber – oh
down to the sea'
it's woodchip and pay packet
soon a scarred desert.
when denuded Mumbulla
will your spirit flee
and what then
oh Mumbulla
when you are departing
will you leave the mountain
in sorrow or rage
and what of the children
oh Mumbulla
the children
and what of the children
and our heritage?

from *The Blackside*, by Kevin Gilbert, Hyland House
Publishing P/L, 1990

Different Realities

Somehow fashioned
from clay and stone
a race apart
a race alone
compelled to write
in legislation
to stop out torture
to curb the hating
while I whom you
deem primitive
knew from birth
to love and live
with all created things
the clay the animals
the rocks and tree
from whence I too
was fashioned formed
by the creator God
to know to keep to be.

from *The Blackside*, by Kevin Gilbert, Hyland House
Publishing P/L, 1990

Child's Dreaming

Within our hands
caress enfold as dreamings flow
to love and teach and guide
the soul and heart
in all the sacred things
that we hold dear
and wisdom in our heritage impart.

from *Child's Dreaming*, by Kevin Gilbert, Hyland House
Publishing P/L, 1992

A Question to God

I know I cannot question Thee
The mighty who hast made the earth and skies
Yet still a tiny voice squeaks from my heart
Squeaks terrified, yet reaching to the skies
'God madest man' and clothed him in his guise
Of colour, features, personnel unique
Yet, God, in wisdom how then wise
In providence – to grant a weak man eyes?
Why eyes? Why colour? Why the ebon'd cross?
So eyes can falsely judge?
And falsely lead vain steps to vain, eternal loss?
Why eyes?
Why? Of all gifts, this magnificence
To be polluted by a lack of love?

from *The Blackside*, by Kevin Gilbert, Hyland House
Publishing P/L, 1990

The Blackside

It's good to be
the Blackside
for we know that in this land
the fire-hardened tree survives
where others – yew and poplars
the fir and mighty oak
have never quiet adapted
to the heat and fire and smoke.

It's good to be the Blackside
fitting in with nature's plan
where she selected colour
for this masterpiece of land
and blended it superbly
with strokes of loving care
for each country has its colour
stark and strong and naked, bare.

It's good to be the Blackside
even though externals change
we tallow-wood and ironbark
are native, that's our point:
imported trees are alien
and the fairest English rose
even after generations
still remains an English rose.

It's good to be
the Blackside
when there's justice on our side
empowered by the spirit
and a firm and humble pride
in being on the Blackside
with nature and her might
the Blackside is the rightside
for this land: the colour's right.

from *The Blackside*, by Kevin Gilbert, Hyland House
Publishing P/L, 1990

The Gurindji

Poor fellow
Simple fellow
Sweet fellow
　　　Strong
Sittin' in the desert
Singin' desert song
Cryin' countin' chickens
Chickens made of lan'
My fellow
Daddy fellow
Right fellow
　　　Land
Sittin' in Australia
Hold your father's land
Ghosts in the ghost gums
Ghosts of tribal band
Sad fellow
Silly fellow
Poor fellow
　　　Clan
Try try simplify
Try to understand
Cryin' countin' chickens
Faces sad and long
Cry cry gibbet me
Me too I bi'long
Me fellow
Little fellow
Good fellow
　　　Men
Cryin' countin' chickens
One eight nine an' ten
Scratch 'im up
Plough 'im up
Chicken same all hen
Gibbit lan' I makim strong
When mines is mines again
Poor fellow
Simple fellow

Sad fellow
     Beg
He bin forgittin'
White man broke the egg
No little chicken fellow
No more fellow hen
Gubbah★ he not gibbit fellow
He take all an' then
When all an' all is taken
Makes all arid plain again.
Says I not gibbit what I stole
I spit upon your dead
Poor fellow
Silly fellow
Sad fellow
     Cry
White fellow gibbit lan'
To hide you when you die.

from *The Blackside*, by Kevin Gilbert, Hyland House
Publishing P/L, 1990

★Gubbah: white man.

A Mother's Appeal to An Artist

Yes
You can help
My boy can sketch cartoons
And other funny things
Can draw real good
And faces like Madonnas carved from ivory wood
Yes you can help if help you will
To teach my boy some finer things
Than 'mission' life where every day
Sees every man despairing
They get drunk as hell
There's nothing else.

Though I can read and I can write
I've never had the chance
I'll fight
For *all* me kids and ten I had
But Balbo is my youngest
Lad
You've *got* to help
He draws real good
Madonnas carved from ivory wood
He goes to school
He's black like me

But *he* can sketch
If you'll just see
His cartoon faces
He sketched *me*
Photo-like
He's *gifted*
But
He's black
There's nothing else.

from *The Blackside*, by Kevin Gilbert, Hyland House
Publishing P/L, 1990

Song to an Unrecognised National Hero: Alice Briggs of Purfleet

There'll be no more roses
for Alice
black Alice
red gum-tips
or fine maidenhair
no grevillea no boronia
for Alice
black Alice
for Alice
no longer is there

There'll be no Land Rights
for Alice
our Alice
except a small space
in the ground
there'll be no saluting
our Alice
black Alice
for Alice is no longer around

Today I visited Alice
our Alice
Alice so loving and brave
the gum-trees were whispering
Alice is here now
as I dropped a waratah
a red waratah
her own waratah
on her grave.

from *The Blackside*, by Kevin Gilbert, Hyland House
Publishing P/L, 1990

Not Choosing

Give me the price of a drink
Brother
Give me – in God's fervent name
To hide out the past and the night
Brother
To block out my loneliness, pain
Give me the price, in Christ's mercy
Hide from me what I've become
Blight out my shame – me a beggar!
Joe Nulinja ... 'bludger' and 'bum'
Been through the mill and I've lost
Brother
Help me to brief out the hurt
Spare me my hurt – and a coin
Brother
Don't walk past, don't treat me like dirt!
The wine of God's mercy flows freely
The banks of the Jordan are near
Help me to stagger on mindless
Forgetting the hell I've ached·here
Gimme the price of some plonk
Brother
'White lady'★ white metho despair
I too am part of the price, brother
The price that has battered me here.
Give it and spare me the pain brother
Of repugnance in your burning eyes
I'm not drunk by choice, I'm a Black
Brother
Escaping the hate I despise
If I wanted to be drunk by choice
Brother
And lie in the gutter out there
Not because I'm a Blackman, but choosing
Then you'd be entitled to sneer.

from *The Blackside*, by Kevin Gilbert, Hyland House
Publishing P/L, 1990

★White lady: methylated spirits

Kiacatoo

On the banks of the Lachlan they caught us
at a place called Kiacatoo
we gathered by campfires at sunset
when we heard the death-cry of curlew
women gathered the children around them
men reached for their nulla and spear
the curlew again gave the warning
of footsteps of death drawing near
Barjoola whirled high in the firelight
and casting his spear screamed out 'Run!'
his body scorched quickly on embers
knocked down by the shot of a gun
the screaming curlew's piercing whistle
was drowned by the thunder of shot
men women and child fell in mid–flight
and a voice shouted 'We've bagged the lot'
and singly the shots echoed later
to quieten each body that stirred
above the gurgling and bleeding
a nervous man's laugh could be heard
'They're cunning this lot, guard the river'
they shot until all swimmers sank
but they didn't see Djarrmal's family
hide in the lee of the bank
Djarrmal warned 'Stay quiet or perish
they're cutting us down like wild dogs
put reeds in your mouth – underwater
we'll float out of here under logs'
a shot cracked and splintered the timber
the young girl Kalara clutched breath
she later became my great grandma
and told the story of my people's death

The Yoorung bird cries by that place now
no big fish will swim in that hole
my people pass by that place quickly
in fear with a quivering soul
at night when the white ones are sleeping
content in their modern day dreams
we hurry past Kiacatoo
where we still hear the shuddering screams

you say 'Sing me no songs of past history
let us no further discuss'
but the question remains still unanswered
How can you deny us like Pilate
refusing the rights due to us.
The land is now all allocated
the Crown's common seal is a shroud
to cover the land thefts and the murder
but can't silence the dreams of the proud.

from *Inside Black Australia*, edited by Kevin Gilbert, Penguin,
1989

Aboriginal Query

What is it you want
Whiteman?
What do you need from me?
You have taken my life
My culture
My dreams
You have leached the substance
Of love from my being
You have leached the substance
Of race from my loins
Why do you persist?
Is it because you are a child
Whose callous inquisitiveness probes
As a finger questing
To wreck a cocoon
To find the chrysalis inside
To find
To explore
To break open
To learn anew
That nothing new is learned
And like a child
With all a child's brutality
Throw the broken chrysalis to the ground
Then run unthinking
To pull asunder the next
What do you seek?
Why do you destroy me
Whiteman?
Why do you destroy that
Which you cannot hope to understand ...

from *The Blackside*, by Kevin Gilbert, Hyland House
Publishing P/L, 1990

Night flight

Isn't it beautiful
homes twinkle below
out on the horizon
ships quietly glow
isn't it wonderful
being alive
here in the clouds
man filled with his drive
has flown to such heights
that it surely please God
but down on the ground still
you feel the beast plod
surely we marvel
these things we attain
technologically speaking
would make us refrain
from the chasms and passions
rampant down there —
from the base and the coarse
and our ego's sharp snare
yet we grow and there's growth
to'ard the God-state we seek
in time terms infinitesimal
our steps to that peak
the mad and the crazy
religious or sane
on God's endless treadmill
walk on — on again.
We grind on quite mindless
and blinded it seems a series of shadows
and staccato dreams
with flashes of essence
of spirit of flood
we evolve and
emerge from our
substance — our mud
to wallow like buffalo
feet bogged in the flood
our hearts brimmed with anger
our eyes filled with blood

computers all programmed
to save effort, breath
push-button warfare
and opting for death

Isn't it wonderful
lights twinkle below
technologically speaking
the world sure will glow.

from *Black from the Edge*, by Kevin Gilbert, Hyland House
Publishing P/L, 1994

Corroboree

Whereaway oh Coontajerra
whereaway oh Cooraki
do you go to join your brothers
on the bora
by the sea
there to paint yourselves with mourning
ochred sadness setting free
shackled spirits of your fathers
come to dance again with thee.

Whirling high to beating kylies★
and the thump of stamping feet
while didjeridoos are dreeing
to the weird outlandish beat
spirits come to give the warning
or perhaps to laugh in glee
once again the tribe has gathered
on the bora
by the sea

Whereaway oh Coontajerra
whereaway oh Cooraki
dancing love songs
with your people
sharing with your family.

from *The Blackside*, by Kevin Gilbert, Hyland House
Publishing P/L, 1990

★kylies: tapsticks

Tree

I am the tree
the lean hard hungry land
the crow and eagle
sun and moon and sea
I am the sacred clay
which forms the base
the grasses vines and man
I am all things created
I am you and
you are nothing
but through me the tree
you are
and nothing comes to me
except through that one living gateway
to be free
and you are nothing yet
for all creation
earth and God and man
is nothing
until they fuse
and become a total sum of something
together fuse to consciousness of all
and every sacred part aware
alive in true affinity.

from *Inside Black Australia*, edited by Kevin Gilbert, Penguin,
1989

The New True Anthem

Despite what Dorothea has said
about the sun scorched land
you've never really loved her
nor sought to make her grand
you pollute all the rivers
and litter every road
your barbaric graffitti
cut scars where tall trees grow
the beaches and the mountains
are covered with your shame
injustice rules supremely
despite your claims to fame
the mud polluted rivers
are fenced off from the gaze
of travellers and the thirsty
for foreign hooves to graze
a tyranny now rules your soul
to your own image blind
a callousness and uncouth ways
now hallmarks of your kind

Australia oh Australia
you could stand proud and free
we weep in bitter anguish
at your hate and tyranny
the scarred black bodies writhing
humanity locked in chains
land theft and racial murder
you boast on of your gains
in woodchip and uranium
the anguished death you spread
will leave the children of the land
a heritage that's dead

Australia oh Australia
you could stand tall and free
we weep in bitter anguish
at your hate and tyranny.

from *Inside Black Australia*, edited by Kevin Gilbert, Penguin,
1989

The work of other poets

The following fifteen poems by thirteen Aboriginal authors have been selected from *Inside Black Australia: An Anthology of Contemporary Aboriginal Poetry*, edited by Kevin Gilbert, Penguin, 1989.

Sorry

I crawled in.
It was low and dark.
The rocks hung down like teeth.
Teeth that tried to bite.
Teeth that tried to keep the paintings safe.

I lay on my back.
It was too low to sit up.
Marlu jumped across the roof,
Snakes slithered,
Goanna ran,
Emu strutted.

I thought who put these here?
Who painted them with brush of chewn stick,
Some red, some white, some brown, some black?
Long ago they put them here . . .
Those old Nyiyapali men.
Long ago, now this is all that's left.

Gone are those proud hunters, the women digging mata.
Their language, their dance and song.
All that is left of a people now
Tiny painted animals.

SORRY!

Julie Watson Nungarrayi

Julie Watson Nungarrayi is a teacher's aide at a dual-language school in the Northern Territory. She speaks and reads to the children in their own language, Warlpiri.

Soul Music

Dancing to vibrations of unheard melodies
Swaying to the sound of silence in his ears
The deaf man danced alone.
People hearing, laughed
'Poor bastard', they cried. 'He doesn't even know,
The music stopped, long long ago!'
The deaf man kept on dancing
Laughing to himself
'If only they would listen, if only they could know,
How it feels to hear the music
Real music.
The music of your soul!'

Stephen Clayton

Stephen Clayton is of the Wiradjuri people of
central New South Wales. He is employed by
the Health Commission and is involved in
Aboriginal youth and community work.

Red

Red is the colour
of my Blood;
of the earth,
of which I am a part;
of the sun as it rises, or sets,
of which I am a part;
of the blood
of the animals,
of which I am a part;
of the flowers, like the waratah,
of the twining pea,
of which I am a part;
of the blood of the tree
of which I am a part.
For all things are a part of me,
and I am a part of them.

W. Les Russell

W. Les Russell, a published poet, worked for
ten years with the Victorian Department of
Education before taking on a heavy workload of
black community issues in areas Australia-wide.
He has been instrumental in securing the legal
right for Aborigines to question and in some
cases halt the activities of mining and land-
developing corporations.

Municipal Gum

Gumtree in the city street,
Hard bitumen around your feet,
Rather you should be
In the cool world of leafy forest halls
And wild bird calls.
Here you seem to me
Like that poor cart-horse
Castrated, broken, a thing wronged,
Strapped and buckled, its hell prolonged,
Whose hung head and listless mien express
Its hopelessness.
Municipal gum, it is dolorous
To see you thus
Set in your black grass of bitumen –
O fellow citizen,
What have they done to us?

Oodgeroo Noonuccal

Oodgeroo Noonuccal (Kath Walker) was the first Aboriginal author to have a book published. Her poetry book, *We are Going,* was widely acclaimed. Her ensuing publications, which included *Father Sky and Mother Earth* and *My People,* together with her many personal appearances, helped a great deal to create the present national and international focus on Aboriginal issues. Oodgeroo held several senior government positions, spanning thirty years, in her determined effort to gain the social and political changes needed for her people.

The First-born

Where are my first-born, said the brown land, sighing;
They came out of my womb long, long ago.
They were formed of my dust – why, why are they crying
And the light of their being barely aglow?

I strain my ears for the sound of their laughter.
Where are the laws and the legends I gave?
Tell me what happened, you whom I bore after.
Now only their spirits dwell in the caves.

You are silent, you cringe from replying.
A question is there, like a blow on the face.
The answer is there when I look at the dying,
At the death and neglect of my dark, proud race.

Jack Davis

Jack Davis, from Western Australia, has spent a lifetime crusading for Aboriginal causes. To this end he has used his considerable literary talent with great effect. He is an internationally known playwright and poet, having published several books including *The First Born* (poetry) and *The Dreamers* (drama). His play, *No Sugar,* received standing ovations all around Australia and as far afield as Vancouver and Edinburgh. Through his involvement with the Aboriginal Arts Board he has been able to encourage and assist many other Aboriginal writers.

Spiritual song of the Aborigine

I am a child of the Dreamtime People
Part of this Land, like the gnarled gumtree
I am the river, softly singing
Chanting our songs on my way to the sea
My spirit is the dust-devils
Mirages, that dance on the plain
I'm the snow, the wind and the falling rain
I'm part of the rocks and the red desert earth
Red as the blood that flows in my veins
I am eagle, crow and snake that glides
Through the rain-forest that clings to the mountainside
I awakened here when the earth was new
There was emu, wombat, kangaroo
No other man of a different hue
I am this land
And this land is me
I am Australia.

Hyllus Maris

Hyllus Maris joined Sonia Berg to write the award-winning television series 'Women of the Sun'. She also wrote several books for children. Hyllus died at an early age from cancer. Her vision for justice was strong and clear, and it lives on through her writings.

Black Child

Black child's soft mouth atremble,
Angry tears in innocent eyes,
Agony in a mother's heart,
As they hear the white man's lies.
Black child is hurt, and puzzled.
'But Mother loves you, Son', she cries.
But all a mother's love can't dry
The tears in a black child's eyes.
Child grows older, and he's off to school
Mother waves her babe goodbye,
Faltering smile upon her lips,
But tears shine in her eyes.
And there's anger in a brother's fists
And shame in a father's heart,
That he sees his people suffer so,
And a black child's world fall apart.
And he sees all the black man's truths,
Distorted by white man's lies
Poor innocent, helpless, wounded babes.
With tears in their big dark eyes.
Oh, I'd cut out my heart and lay at your feet.
And I'd rip the stars from the blue,
I'd spit on the sun and put out its light,
If I could keep all this hurt from you.
Flesh of my flesh,
And blood of my blood,
You never hear how my aching heart cries,
To a people too cruel,
Too blind to see,
The tears in a black child's eyes.

These breasts can fill and overflow,
They've suckled babies, watched them grow,
This womb, too, has given birth,
How dare you, then, to judge my worth.

By all the gods and powers that be,
That made woman and man,
You and yes, me,
Till they create another human race,
I spit, defiant, in your face,
Though you watch me die as you have done.
I will live again, in my daughers, my sons.
And you will hear my cry, even as you deny,
I, too, am human.
I'd spit on the sun and put out its light,
If I could keep all this hurt from you.
Flesh of my flesh,
And blood of my blood,
You never hear how my aching heart cries,
To a people too cruel,
Too blind to see,
The tears in a black child's eyes.

Maureen Watson

Memo To J.C.

When you were down here JC and walked this earth,
You were a pretty decent sort of bloke,
Although you never owned nothing, but the clothes on your
   back,
And you were always walking round, broke.
But you could talk to people, and you didn't have to judge,
You didn't mind helping the down and out
But these fellows preaching now in your Holy name,
Just what are they on about?
Didn't you tell these fellow to do other things,
Besides all that preaching and praying?
Well, listen, JC, there's some things ought to be said,
And I might as well get on with the saying.
Didn't you tell them 'don't judge your fellow man'
And 'love ye one another'
And 'not put your faith in worldly goods'.
Well, you should see the goods that they got, brother!
They got great big buildings and works of art,
And millions of dollars in real estate,
They got no time to care about human beings,
They forgot what you told 'em, mate;
Things like, 'Whatever ye do to the least of my brothers,
Things ye do also unto me',
Yeah, well these people who are using your good name,
They're abusing it, JC,
But there's people still living the way you lived,
And still copping the hyprocrisy, racism and hate,
Getting crucified by the fat cats, too,
But they don't call us religious, mate.
Tho' we got the same basic values that you lived by,
Sharin' and carin' about each other,
And the bread and the wine that you passed around,
Well, we're still doing that, brother.
Yeah, we share our food and drink and shelter,
Our grief, our happiness, our hopes and plans,
But they don't call us 'Followers of Jesus',
They call us black fellas, man.

But if you're still offering your hand in forgiveness
To the one who's done wrong, and is sorry,
I reckon we'll meet up later on,
And I got no cause to worry.
Just don't seem right somehow, that all the good you did,
That people preach, not practise, what you said,
I wonder, if it all died with you, that day on the cross,
And if it just never got raised from the dead.

Maureen Watson

Maureen Watson travels extensively within
Australia and overseas. She is an accomplished
actress and poet as well as being a gifted
storyteller. She comes from a large family well
known in Queensland and New South Wales
for their care and active participation in the
drive for a more positive change in Aboriginal
politics and freedoms.

Lament for a Dialect

Dyirringan is lost to the tribes of the Yuin,
    I am filled with remorse and I weep at the ruin
O beautiful words that were softly spoken,
    Now lay in the past, all shattered and broken,
We forgot it somehow when English began,
    The sweet sounding dialect of Dyirringan.
If we're to be civilised whom can we blame,
    To have lost you, my language, is my greatest shame.

Mary Duroux

Mary Duroux is of the Thungutti people of northern New South Wales. She is a recognised artist and has worked in several different Aboriginal cooperatives in the Kempsey area of New South Wales.

Okay, Let's Be Honest

Okay, let's be honest:
I ain't no saint,
but then again,
I wasn't born in heaven.
Okay, Okay!
So let's be honest:
I've been in and out.
since the age of eleven.

And I've been mean,
        hateful
          and downright dangerous.
I've lain in my own blood
in hotels
boys' homes,
and cop shops.
I've cursed my skin:
not black, not white.
Just another non-identity,
fighting to be Mr. Tops.

Yeah, so I'm called a bastard,
an animal, a trouble maker,
while my accusers watch my brothers smashed,
thrown into dog-boxes drunk, crying for the dreamtime
My memory is still wet with my mother's tears,
flowing by my father's grave.
Just another black family
alone and lost in the race for a dime.

As early as I can remember,
I was made aware of my differences,
and slowly my pains educated me:
either fight or lose.
'One Sided', I hear you say.
Then come erase the scars from my brain,
and show me the other side of your face:
the one with the smile painted on with the colours
    of our sacred land you abuse.

'One Sided?' Yeah mate!
Cop it sweet 'n all.

'After all, you stepped out of line
and got caught.
So take it easy,' you say,
'You're not like the rest.
You have got brains and a bright future,
there's no battle to be fought.'

But that don't tell me what I want to know.
So tell me: why do we have to stand in line?
Why do we have to live your way, in subtle slavery
to earn the things that once were free?
Why do I have to close my eyes,
and make believe I cannot see
just what you are doing:
to my people – *OUR PEOPLE* – and me?

Well, bloody hell, Mate!
It ain't one sided at all!
Come read the loneliness and confusion
on the walls of this cell of seven by eleven.
Yeah, okay, I'll be honest:
I ain't no saint.
But then again,
I SURE WASN'T BORN IN HEAVEN!

Robert Walker

Life Is Life

The rose among thorns
may not feel the sun's kiss each mornin'
and though it is forced to steal the sunshine
stored in the branches by those who cast shadows,
it is a rose and it lives.

Robert Walker

Robert Walker was born on Point Pearce Aboriginal Mission in Yorke Peninsula on Christmas Day 1958. As a poet he sought answers to universally asked questions on human rights as well as the callous indifference of whites and white law, which he personally experienced throughout his life. Robert Walker died in custody in Freemantle jail aged twenty-five. He died somewhere before 5 a.m. on 28 August 1984, the direct result of a prolonged and vicious beating. Forty-one other prisoners gave documented evidence to this effect, but no charges were ever laid against the officers responsible. The fact of his death along with all other Aboriginal deaths in custody remains an as yet unanswered cry for justice and humanity.

Remember?

Born by river
Gently rested on a lily pad
Woman   tired eyes
Wading beside filling string bag with lily roots,
  fish, small tortoise, buds
Woman – singing

Around fire, night time sitting
With Kin – sharing food
   cooked in hot ashes
Children laughing,
   Mother singing
 baby on breast
Women telling stories, sharing, giving
Songs, spirit names, teaching
  IN LANGUAGE.

No more river – Big dam now
String bag empty
   Supermarket now
Women sitting in big houses
   sharing, singing, remembering
   Mother crying, baby clinging
Women telling stories,
  new stories, new names
   NEW LANGUAGE . . .

        Eva Johnson

Eva Johnson was born at Daly River, Northern Territory. She was raised in a mission after being forcibly taken from her mother by the Aboriginal Protection Board. Eva now has a Bachelor of Arts degree with a major in drama. She wrote and co-directed the play *Tjindarella*, which is available on video.

Night Marauders

A campfire emits an embered glow
And soft sea-breezes gently blow
In the cool of a north Australian night,
Where lies a sleeping Black village – calm and quiet.

The scene is peaceful, sedate and serene.
There's no threat of danger or doom foreseen.
Then, all at once with a shrieking yell
Come night marauders
Like fiendish demons from hell.

Into the village they come at the run
Armed with the shackle and the upraised gun.
On they rush like a human sea
Shooting and killing and laughing with glee.

The blacks grab their babies
And try to take flight
But are subdued and shackled
By the fiends of the night.
Then dragged by their chains to the village compound
While their houses are burned – burned to the ground.

Black women are wailing,
Their children are crying,
Their men are bound helpless
And the village is slowing dying.

Gerry Bostock

Gerry Bostock is of the Bandjalong people of
Grafton, New South Wales. He gave his support
to Kevin Gilbert and the other Aboriginal
patriots who organised the Tent Embassy in
1972. (The Tent Embassy, on the lawns in front
of Parliament House in Canberra, mightily
raised Aboriginal awareness within the general

community and paved the way for much-needed political reforms.) Gerry has since travelled overseas with Aboriginal delegations, written articles and poetry and been involved in making several Aboriginal television productions, including 'Threshold', 'The Land My Mother' and 'Lousy Little Sixpence'.

Who Owns Darling Street?

Whiteman dressed in your fancy clothes
I'm laughing at you as you look down your nose
And sign your petitions to keep out the Blacks
Call us lazy bludgers who live off your tax
You say we're the cause of this Black and White strife
But white backstabber you don't hurt me with your knife
For though we're the Blacks you love to ill-treat
Let me ask you Whiteman, who owns Darling Street?

Whiteman you came such a short while ago
Erecting your fences where once wildlife roamed
Draining natural resources with your cattle and sheep
Abusing the land by playing for keeps
Your thirst for land and your love for money
Makes me laugh at you Whiteman as I think it's funny
Really it is, don't we have more right
To sign a petition to keep out the whites?

So think it over Whiteman you're wrong again
And all your petitions don't mean a thing
For though we're the Blacks you love to ill-treat
Let me ask you Whiteman, who owns Darling Street?

Frank Doolan

Frank Doolan belongs to the Kamilaroi group of
northern New South Wales. In transitional times
the Kamilaroi were a powerful force in opposing
the early invasion and colonisation of their area.
Frank is tertiary-educated and has written a great
deal of poetry. Although he has a gentle,
sensitive spirit there is evidence of the kind of
strength displayed by his ancestors; that is, he is
prepared to challenge tyranny whatever the odds
against him might be!

Mary's plea

Where am I
You, my people
Where am I standing.
Take me back
   and hold my hand
I want to be with you.
I want to smell
      the smoke
         of burnt grass.

Where are you
      my people
I am lost;
I've lost everything, my culture
      that should be my own.

Where am I
The clouds
      o'er shadow me
         but my memories are there.
But I am lost,
   my people,
Take me back
And teach the things
I want to learn.

Is it really you my people,
The voices,
The soft voices that I hear.

Daisy Utemorrah

Daisy Utemorrah is of the Ngarinjin people
from the Kimberley area. She is a literacy
teacher and a health worker. She has a detailed
knowledge of Ngarinjin traditions, and writes
and tells stories concerning them.

The Wiradjuri people of New South Wales- their language

Who were the Wiradjuri?

White colonists first came to the Wiradjuri area in the 1830s. At this time the members of the Wiradjuri numbered from ten thousand to twenty thousand. They were a nation in themselves, self-sufficient in every way. The people were secure in their spiritual and cultural adherence, and their way of life was ecologically sound.

Within fifty years of white settlement in their area almost two-thirds of the original population lay dead, and it had become totally impossible for those left to maintain any semblance of their previous culture and lifestyle. At this time, the survivors, the remnants of this once proud nation, were taken — some in chains — to various missions which had been set up in the area. Although these were desperate, despairing years for the Wiradjuri people, their survival spirit was never vanquished. The Wiradjuri spirit is indeed very much a part of the overall contemporary reawakening of the Aboriginal community as a whole.

Many Wiradjuri people today hold high-profile positions in the law and politics of Australia, in education, in many areas of sport and many other spheres of Australian life. Some among the Wiradjuri who have been politically prominent are Jack Ferguson, Pearl Gibbs, Kevin Gilbert and Paul Coe. Paul Coe was the 1990 Aboriginal representative to the Human Rights Commission in Geneva, and for the past two years he has been the Indigenous Peoples elected spokesman to the United Nations. The fact that Paul Coe enjoys such international recognition is an honour for all Australians.

Words from the Wiradjuri dialects

adelong	a plain near a river
allaway	rest or stay here; sit down
amaroo	a beautiful place
arakoon	hardwood fighting shield
arana	the moon
baanbaan	ripples on water, raised by the wind
baddawal	the Wiradjuri word for boomerang
baiyai	a meeting place of two parties; a tryst
balargorang	a place where the kangaroos feed
balbu	kangaroo rat
baldry;	
baiderodgery	a small plover
ballagirin	an old possum
ballanda	the early Dreaming before people were created
ballarra	spear barbs
ballima	a long way off; very far away
ballina;	
balloona	fighting ground; blood running from the wounded
ballowrie	lily
balliran;	
billiran	the silence of the night
ballugan	animals
balwandara	to swim, to float
bangaroo	koala
bangayarra	to reconcile
bangolong	autumn
baradine	red wallaby
barbigal	frosty place
barellan	the meeting of waters
barramalinga	convalescent
barrawinga	to hunt
barringun	dead fish in a creek
baryugil	a large lizard
bearbung	to camp near a creek
bedgeribong	a big gum tree near the river
belabula	a stony river

belah;	
belar	the place of forest oaks
berralunya	a white-crested crane
bibboorah	sun setting behind a hill; looks like fire
bibburah	a fire in the distance
bilimari	down a mountain towards a river
bimbi	a place of many birds
bimble;	
bembil	a box tree
binalong	towards a high place
binni; binnia;	
birriwa; birriwel	courage, bravery
binge	belly
birramal	bush
birrawanna	to descend
bocable	sheep jumping as they go through a gate (innovated after 1830)
bokhara	wearing a skin cloak
bogan	the birthplace of a great man
bogonk	a large moth
boona	swampy country
boorongong	bitter-tasting water
boorooma	a dingo
boree	fire
boridgeree	a big waterhole
brewarrina	a clump of wattle trees; two people standing; a place where wild gooseberries grow
brewongle	a good place to camp
brolgan; brolga	the brolga bird, often called a native companion
buckinguy	a place where cooking is done
buddah	tree
budgeriga;	
gidgerrago	a small grass parrot
bugaldie	the home of a death adder
bulah	two
bulgandramine	an Aborigine holding a boomerang
bumanna	to move with the wings of a bird
bumbaldry	the noise of people jumping into water
bunyip	a mythical amphibious monster
burgooney	ants tunnelling in sandy country
burrago	stagnant water
burrambim	eternal

burrandong	fur-covered animals
burrangong	good fishing area
burringar	an especially long boomerang
burrowa	a plains turkey
buyuma	the foot of a hill
byamee; baiame;	
biami	supreme spiritual being
bygalorie	a red kangaroo
bywong	a big hill
canberra;	
ka-amberra;	
canberry	a meeting place
cannonba	the place of shingle-back lizards
canobolas	two shoulders
canowindra	home
carawandoo	plenty of birds come and drink here
carcoar	a frog
cargellico	a lake
carinda	you carry it
cobar; cuburra	red pigment; burnt earth
cobbadah	a certain place on a hill
cobbora	the head
colah; coolah	anger
colane	a type of tree
collendina; collerina	floods
collie	a lagoon or waterhole
comara	to cut a sinew
combara	women in terror near a waterhole
comboyne	a female
condobolin	a hop (herbal) bush
cookamidgera	many stumps of trees by a creek
coonabarabran	an inquisitive person
coonamble;	
goonamble	plenty of dirt
cootamundra;	
gooramundra	a low-lying place
cooyal	hot like a fire
coradgery	the land at the head of the Bogan River
corella; corinella	one pink and white parrot
cowra	eagle on a rock; many rocks
corroboree	a special dance, a part of sacred ceremonies

corrodgery	sandy country
crudine	a goanna
cuban	jammed between two trees
cudgegong	the red clay used to decorate the body; a red-earthed hill
cudal	flat
cumberoona	a river running through a deep gorge
cumbingum;	
cumbijowa	a runaway woman
cumboogie;	
cumboogle	sweet-scented gum leaves
comboorah	gum trees near a sacred site
curra	a fresh spring
currawang;	
currawong	a tree used to make wooden implements
currawarna	pine trees
dandaloo	a big storm; hail
dandarbong	very pretty
dangunyah	to visit; come here
daroobalgie	to jump or dive into water
derribong	green trees
dillabirra	to scatter
dindima	a group of stars
dirigeree	willy-wagtail
dironbirong	the sun shining red on the clouds in the evening (sunset)
dubbo; thubbo	a head covering
dungog; tungog	easy to see hills
eerawai	mirage
ellimatta	our dwelling
elouera	a pleasant place to camp
erowari	clouds
eugowra	where the sand washes down from the hills
eumungerie	trees
euriowie	a waterhole
euruderie	a single tree
galong	a flying fox
ganmain	a man decorated with scars

garema	a place to camp
gariwang	cold east wind
gerogery	a pleasant place
gibber	rocks
gilgandra	a long waterhole
gilgooma	house of the white man
gillamagong	house of a very rich white man
girilambone	a place of many stars; where a star fell
girraween	a quiet place with many pretty flowers
girrilang	a star
giwarra	to cook
goimbla	a lot of hills
gong	water; running
goodooga	a big lagoon
goola	a kangaroo
gooloo	where you find something special
gooloogong	where you find running water
gowrie	the down of a bird's breast
grawlin; grawin	a large plain
guabinga	to rest or sit down for a while
gunaga; gunawyle	a group of waterholes
gungarman	a swampy area
gunguari	a halo; a circle around the moon
gunyah	a shelter made of bark and branches
gurawin	a flower
gurawoong	a bandicoot
gurda	in the cool of the evening
gurian	a lake or lagoon
guya; kuya	fish
indubilla	you two
ingar	crayfish
inglebar	crayfish holes
iraga	spring (the season)
iraidurai	the morning star
irambang	a steep dangerous mountain
iramir	steep riverbank; any precipice
iremillan	at dawn
irinirin	cold west wind
ironmongie	a large white ant
irribin	a swallow

jarara	a rock with water flowing over it
jemalong	a platypus
jerrabung	an old man
kadina	lizards on a plain
kadungle	a small lizard
kalianna	to ascend
kalindy	an island
kallargang	edible roots, yams
kallindalein	a black snake
kalmaldain	a composer/choreographer (responsible for corroborees)
kara kara	the moon
karana	a quiet place
karawatha	a place of pine trees
kariwang	a leaf
karrari	a fishing net
kiacatoo	a flowing river (the river known today as the Lachlan)
kinamindi	to laugh
kindaimanna	to play, have fun
kobbadah	an underground spring in a hilly area
koimblah	red
kookamidgera	many stumps of trees by a creek
kula	trees; timber; firewood
kulamon; coolamon;	
kulomin	a wooden container
kullingral	a deep waterhole
long	a flat area of land
lowanna	a young girl
maldanna	to provide something
malduringa	to dig for edible roots
mandagery	a chain of waterholes in a creek
mandurama	waterholes
manildra	a place near water
mara	a black duck
marara	to stop
marragarra	to hold on tightly
mawamball	men meeting together
mebbin	a male
merri	a tame dingo

merribinda	a place where a dingo goes to drink
merrigang; merrigonary	a place where dingoes are found
miandetta	a bend in a river
mil	an eye
mil-mil	many eyes (watching)
milbrulong	a rosella
mildura	a place where people have sore eyes
millawelang	a special bush
millbarra	to beat out a rhythm with clapsticks
milparinka	to search and find a waterhole
minimbah	the home of a teacher
minore	the place where it is
mogo	a stone axe
mogong	to sharpen stone axes near water
molong	a rocky area
mudah; mudall	breasts
mulgabirra	to give everything
mullyandry; mullian	an eagle hawk
mumble; mumbil	a black-timbered wattle tree
mungeribah	red clay
muogamarra	to keep in reserve for future use
murramirra	to be surprised
murramurang	someone who is always laughing
murranal	blind
murrarogan	a frost
murrarundi	five fingers
murrawarra	to stand one's ground
murray	goes quickly
murriang	the sky world where Byamee, the great creator, lives
murrobo	thunder
murrua	westerly wind
murrumborah	two canoes on the way to the bora ground
murrungoyarra	for ever and ever
myamley	to talk with someone while in a hut
na	to see
nalleghee	our
nanara	a black snake
nanardine	swallow
nandirong	bent like a hook
nangar	a cliff face; red rocks

nanima; nanimi	something that is lost
narang	little
narbong	a woman's bag; the pouch of a marsupial
nardu	waterlily seeds
narra	something forked, i.e. where two creeks meet or the branches of a tree, etc.
narrabri	a big creek
narraburra	very rough country
narrandera	a forked-tongue lizard
narrawai	heat mist in the air
narromine	a place where you find honey
nelungaloo	many lizards
nioka	a green hill
nirikai	a young woman
nooroo	night time
nulang	mist ascending
nulgarra	bright
nulla nulla	a large-headed wooden club
nullegai	we (the two of us)
nyngan	a place of many streams
nyrang	a little creek
omeo	mountains
oolong	a gathering of brolgas
ooma	an ear ache
oorin	an emu
ootha	an ear
orana	welcome
pindari	high ground
pullabooka	the top one
quabathoo	topknot pigeon
quambone	fog
quandong	a wild fruit, a little like a peach
quandialla; wombialla	a porcupine
quidong	a place of echo; a cold place
quipolly	waterholes containing fish
tabulam	my natural home
talara	frost or snow

tallarook	honeysucker (bird)
tallawalla	forest country
tallawang	a wild apple
taloumbi	a windy place
tarana	a large waterhole
terramungamine	a man with a broken thigh
thuddungra	where water rushes down
tillabudgery	a good view or lookout
tomanbill	crooked timber
tomingley	death adder
toogong	a smoky fire near water
toongi	a scrub turkey
toora weena	plenty of brown snakes
towradgi	the keeper of sacred stones
trajere	a place where sacred stones are kept
trangie	quick
tubbul	a bore (underground water)
tugrabakl	a place of ironbark trees
tullibigeal	a wooden-headed spear
ty-agong	a wombat
uambi	a pine scrub
uardry	a yellow box tree
ulamamibri	a place where possums breed
ulinga	to fly
ullailinga	to call for someone
uloola	sun
ululu	a whistling duck (the name comes from the noise they make as they fly)
ulmara	a bend in the river
urana	the noise of a flying quail
urimbirra	to take care of something
wangin; wagin;	
waugin	a crow
wagin wagin	many crows
wagga-wagga	a sick or dizzy man
wahroonga	our home
walmer	to carry a heavy load
walla	a waterhole in a rock
walla walla	much rain

wallangara;	
wyangula	a large amount of water
wallaru	a small mountain kangaroo
wallaumarra	to protect as a guardian
wallenbeen	stony hill
wallerawang	always plenty of water
wambangalong	plenty of grey kangaroos
wambinga	to support
wammarra	to build a shelter
wanbidgee	blackfellow
wangian	to sit away from the fire
wangoola	to dig for water
wannanna	to throw
wantabadgery	fighting
waratah	a native shrub (now the floral emblem of New South Wales)
warrah	rain falling
warramba	a turtle
warren	strong
warrialda	a place where wild honey is found
warrimoo	an eagle
warringah	a sign of rain
warri warri	many hills
warroo	a place of hornets
warrumbungle	low mountain range
waugoola	where you'll find clear drinking water
weddin; widden	to stay or remain
weeragulla; wirragulla	many parrots
weetalabah	a scarcity of firewood; the place where the fire went out
wilban	cave
willurai	very sweet
windang	the scene of a fight
winga	to sit down; rest so that one may live
wirrimbah;	
wirrimbirra	to preserve something
wirrinya	sleep
wirong	the north wind
wollar	a flat area by a creek
woomba	evening star

wurinyan	to love
wurli	a shelter
wyong	a spring with running water; a place where Christmas bells grow
yabbi	freshwater crayfish
yalbillinga	to learn
yalgu	leafless tree
yallaradang	gum oozing from trees
yallul	always
yambinya	to live as a husband and wife
yanco	the song of running water
yarea	evening
yarramalong	a place of wild horses
yarrawullai	gum tree blossoms
yarringan	clear, as transparent as water
yawarra	to watch over, or take care of something

A Wiradjuri chant

Mawamball

Mawamball. Mawamball.
Barbigul.   Barbigul.
Irambang.

Pindari. Pindari.
Tillabud, budgery.
Gariwang.

Na, wambangalong.
Derribong. Derribong.
Balargorang.

Brewongle.
Bibburah. Bibburah.
Na, wambangalong. Windang.

Men meet together

(The English version of 'Mawamball')

Men meet together, meet together
In a frosty place, a frosty place
On top of a mountain high.

On this high ground, this high ground
They stand and watch
As the cold east wind goes by.

They see many grey kangaroos.
Beneath the gum trees, beneath the trees
The kangaroos feed and lie.

It is a good place to camp.
Make a fire. Make a fire.
We'll fight those kangaroos, by and by.

Two Wiradjuri songs

Noo - roo noo - roo na kar - a kar - a Nall - ee - ghee nar - ang low - ann - a.
Null - e - gai wall au - mar - ra - a Nall - ee - ghee nar - ang low - ann - a.

Wirr - in - ya___ ir - ai - dur - ai___ ir - e mill - an___ tra - ngie tra - ng - ie.
Nall - ee - ghee wedd - in wur - in - yan,___ ball - i - ran ball - i - ran ball - i - ran.

Repeat 1st verse as 3rd verse

The words of 'Na kara-kara' and 'Narang irribin' (overleaf) have been presented with the accompanying music of a familiar melody for the benefit of anyone who might like to sing the Wiradjuri words in a contemporary mode. Traditional Wiradjuri people would have chanted the words.

See the moon

(The English version of 'Na kara-kara')

It's night, it's night, see the moon.
Our little girl is sleeping.
The morning star and
Dawn will come soon.

The two of us will watch over and guard
Our little girl.
We will stay here and love her
In the silence of the night.

It's night, it's night, see the moon.
Our little girl is sleeping.
The morning star and
Dawn will come soon.

Narang irribin

Na-rang na-rang irr-i-bin, na-rang na-rang irr-i-bin
Na-rang na-rang irr-i-bin, na-rang na-rang irr-i-bin

Ir-in ir-in u-ling-a. Bi-rra wa-nna gua-bin-ga
Na ka-ra ka-ra girr-a-lang, ka-ra ka-ra girr-a-lang.

Goo-loo gong ka-ran-a. Goo-loo gong ka-ran-a.
Nu-lang binn-a long u-ling-a. Bi-rra wa-nna gua-bin-ga.

Little swallow

(The English version of 'Narang irribin')

Little swallow
Little swallow
There's a cold west wind.
Fly down and rest awhile
Where you find water and quiet.
Where you find water and quiet.

Little swallow
Little swallow
See the moon and stars
The moon and stars
And the mist rising up high.
Fly down and rest awhile.

INDEX